CW00832096

Ninja Speedi Cookbook for Beginners 2023

Simple and Delicious Recipes for Ninja Speedi Rapid Cooker & Air Fryer to Steam Crisp, Bake and Broil Meals Everyday

Larry Morelli

Table of Content

INTRODUCTION

Ninja Speedi Rapid Cooker and Air Fryer Series is yet another amazing addition to the existing line of multicookers the company has presented to the world. The way Shark Ninja keeps bringing innovation into kitchen technology is simply mind-boggling. The Ninja Speedi rapid cookers do the same. There are two models that are released as a part of the Ninja Speedi series – the SF300 and the SF301. Both models have a smart switch that lets you unlock two different sets of cooking features on a single pot. The SF300 has 10 cooking functions in one, whereas the SF301 model has 12 functions. With that slight change, both appliances work on the same principle, and they have a similar design.

So if you have any of the Ninja Speedi Rapid Cooker's models, then this cookbook will help you create a variety of meals using different cooking methods. This cookbook has all the recipes categorized as per the cooking functions of Ninja Speedi, so now you don't have to go through every recipe to find out how it is cooked. It means that you can directly skip to the Slow Cooker Recipes to make use of the Ninja Speedi's "Slow Cook" function if you like or go to the Air Fry section, the Sous Vide recipes, or others to use the respective functions. Isn't that great?

ABOUT THE NINJA SPEEDI RAPID COOKER

Anyone who likes quick, delectable, and healthy cooking needs the Ninja Speedi Rapid Cooker. This cooker employs its pressurized steam cooking technology to instantly lock in taste while maintaining the greatest amount of nutrients, eliminating the need for pre-cooking or prolonged simmering durations during meal preparation. There are fewer dishes to wash after cooking because of the pot's speedy heating. When steaming vegetables or seafood recipes, it also has a low water capacity that helps prevent food waste.

With the Ninja SF301 Speedi Rapid Cooker & Air Fryer, you can quickly and simply make tasty and healthy family favorites! With its 6-qt size and Speedi Meals feature, you can prepare meals for up to 4 people in one pot in as little as 15 minutes. To steam, crisp, bake, roast, air fry, sear & sauté, slow cook, and more, choose from 12 different modes! Use air fry technology to swiftly maintain moisture and provide a crisp finish with the revolutionary Rapid Cooking system. In your kitchen, you can access thousands of Speedi Meal recipes with customizable ingredients by simply switching between Rapids Cooker mode and Air Fry mode. The nonstick cooking pot and crisper tray are both dishwasher-safe, making cleanup a breeze. With the Ninja SF301 Speedi Rapid Cooker & Air Fryer, cook wholesome meals at home with up to 75% less fat than traditional deep frying and start producing delectable dishes quickly!

Benefits and Features of the Ninja Speedi Rapid Cooker

The Shark Ninja's newest addition to its selection of tiny kitchen appliances is the brand-new Ninja Speedi Rapid Cooker and Air Fryer, which can prepare "restaurant-quality meals from the comfort of your own home." You may simultaneously air fry and steam meals using Ninja's Rapid Cooking System to cut down on meal preparation time and enjoy your dinner. Using the SmartSwitch on the cooker, you may switch between the Air Fry/Stovetop mode, which is great for frozen prepared meals, and the rapid cooker mode, which is great for a whole chicken or turkey roasts, fresh and frozen proteins, and 3-part meals. You have a 6-quart capacity that can hold "up to one pound of spaghetti and up to four chicken breasts simultaneously."

When it comes to compact kitchen appliances, Ninja is one of the most well-known brands, and it is currently expanding its inventory with the brand-new Speedi Rapid Cooker and Air Fryer. The Speedi can cook your family's entire meal in one pot in under 15 minutes. The Ninja Speedi is a versatile kitchen appliance, and it can be used for a variety of cooking modes, such as pressure cooking, sous vide, steam and crisp, slow cooking, sautéing, and more. Some benefits and features of using this cooker include:

Smart Switch

If you look at the top right corner of the Ninja Speedi's lid, you will find a rotatable handle that has "Rapid Cooker and Stovetop" written over it. This handle can be moved up and down to select between the two modes. When you select the Rapid Cooker by keeping the handle pointing upwards, this unlocks the following cooking function on the appliance:

* Speedi Meals * Steam and Crisp

* Steam and Bake   * Steam

* Proof (Only available in SF301 not in SF300 model)

Then you can turn the Smart Switch to the downward position, and you can then unlock the other cooking options like:

* Air Fry* Bake/Roast   * Sear/Sauté   * Slow Cook   * Sous Vide   * Broil

* Dehydrate(Only available in SF301 not in SF300 model)

In this way, without changing or switching the lids, you can turn this appliance into a cooker that pressure cook, steam and crisp, steam, air fry, sous vide, and do so much more.

Adjustable Crisper Tray

Another interesting feature of the Ninja Speedi Rapid Cooker is that the crisper tray that comes with it is adjustable, and you can place it in the bottom position as well as in the raised position. In this way, you can add some ingredients to the bottom of the cooking pot and then place the crisper tray on top in the raised position to cook easy three-part meals.

Speedy Clean Up

The Ninja Speedi Rapid Cooker is not only quick at cooking food, but it also takes less time to clean this appliance. The crisper tray and other removable accessories are dishwashers safe, and you can wash them easily without damaging the coating.

How to Use the Ninja Speedi Rapid Cooker

Take a good look at your appliance before getting started with it. Inside the Ninja Speedi Box, you will find a main unit with a Unit Lid. The unit lid flip opens, and it has a heating element fitted inside. On top of the Unit lid, there is a vent for air, and on the corner, there is a Smart Switch. This lid has a handle on the side for users so they can easily open or close it.

Inside the appliance, there is a 6-quart cooking pot that can be removed and installed back into the device. Then there is a condensation collection that has to be installed at the back of the appliance to collect the vapors. There is a crisper tray that goes into the cooking pot, and it is placed inside when for air frying and crisping food. It can be adjusted for other cooking functions as well.

The Ninja Speedi Rapid Cooker has a relatively easy-to-use control panel. There are three sets of arrows that you can use to adjust the cooking settings. Firstly there is TEMP up and down arrows which are used to increase or decrease the value of temperature for each mode. Then on the other side of the display screen, there is TIME up and down arrows which are used to set the cooking time. Below these arrows, you can see two sets of cooking modes:

* Rapid Cooker * Air Fry/Stovetop

When you rotate the Smart Switch on the lid, either one of those options lights up on the control panel. You can select from the options given under each of them using another set of arrows which are present at the center of the control panel.

Rapid Cooker

When you turn the Smart Switch upwards, it unlocks all the functions that are given under the Rapid Cooker option on the control panel. In this mode, you can pressure cook food through the "Speedi Meals" options. Then you can pair steam with crisping or steam with baking. Then there is a basic steam mode, and finally, if you have the SF301 model, you can also proof your bread using the "proof" cooking function.

Speedi Meals

Before beginning, make sure the Crisper Tray is out of the pot's bottom. Add liquid and ingredients to the bottom of the pot as directed by the instructions. Place the Crisper Tray in the pot in an upright position after removing the legs. As directed by the recipe, add ingredients to the tray. Move the SmartSwitch to Rapid Cooker, then choose Speedi Meals with the center arrows. The predetermined setting will be shown. Then adjust the temperature and time and press the start button to initiate.

To start or stop cooking, press START/STOP. Progress bars on display will show that the machine is gaining steam. The timer will start to count once the unit reaches the proper steam level. The device will beep and show "End" when the cooking time reaches zero. Use the up arrows to the right of the display to add more time if your dish needs it. Preheating is skipped by the device.

Steam & Crisp

According to the recipe, add the ingredients. Switch the SmartSwitch to the Rapid Cooker. Then turn the Smart Switch, select the Steam and Crisp mode, adjust the temperature and time, and press the start button to initiate. To start or stop cooking, press Start/Stop. Progress bars on display will show that the machine is gaining steam. The timer will start to count once the unit reaches the proper steam level.

The device will beep and show "End" when the cooking time reaches zero. Use the up arrow to the right of the display to add more time if your cuisine needs it. Preheating is skipped by the device.

Steam and Bake

Make sure the Crisper Tray is positioned at the bottom. The baking supplies should be put on top of the tray. Move SmartSwitch to Rapid Cooker, then choose Steam & Bake with the center arrows. It will show the current temperature setting. Use the up and down arrows to the left of the display to change the temperature in 10 or 15-degree increments from 250°F to 400°F. To change the cooking time from 1 minute to 1 hour and 15 minutes, in 1-minute increments up to 1 hour, use the up and down arrows to the right of the display.

To start or stop cooking, press Start/Stop. The progress bars on display will show that the unit is building up as. The timer will start counting down after preheating is finished. When the cooking time hits zero, the appliance will move the SmartSwitch to Rapid Cooker and then choose steam using the front center arrows.

In order to get the liquid to boil, the machine will start preheating. Progress bars on display will show that the device is generating steam. The timer will start counting down after preheating is finished. When the appliance achieves temperature, the preheating animation will stop showing, and the timer will start to count down on display.

Proof

Make sure the Crisper Tray is positioned at the bottom. Place the baking accessory on top of the tray after adding dough to it. Move SmartSwitch to Rapid Cooker, then choose PROOF with the front-center arrows. It will show the current temperature setting. Choose a temperature between 90°F and 105°F using the up and down arrows to the left of the display in 5-degree increments. The proof time can be changed from 15 minutes to 4 hours by using the up and down arrows to the right of the display. To start or stop cooking, press Start/Stop. The device will beep and show "End" when the cooking time reaches zero.

Air Fry/Stovetop

By turning the Smart Switch downwards, it will activate the Air Fry/Stovetop mode, which lets you use the following cooking modes. You can air fry, bake/roast, dehydrate, sear/saute, sous vide, and slow cook food using this mode.

Air Fry

Be sure to place the Crisper Tray in the bottom position. Close the lid, then turn the Smart Switch, select the air fry mode, adjust the temperature and time, and press the start button to initiate. When using Air Fry functions, be sure to add an additional 5 minutes to your total cook time to allow for preheat. Add ingredients after the first 5 minutes.

It is advised to shake ingredients occasionally when air frying for the best results. You can shake or toss the contents for even browning after opening the top and lifting out the pot. Close the lid after finishing by lowering the pot back into the appliance. Once the lid is shut, cooking will begin again automatically.

Bake/Roast

Make sure the Crisper Tray is positioned at the bottom. Close the lid, move SmartSwitch to Air Fry/Stovetop, then use the center front arrows to select Bake/Roast. The default temperature setting will display. Use the up and down arrows to the left of the display to choose a temperature from 300°F to 400°F, in either 10 or 15 degree increments. Use the up and down arrows to the right of the display to adjust the cook time up to 1 hour in 1 minute increments and from 1 hour to 4 hours in 5 minute increments. Press START/STOP to begin cooking. Like air fry, the Bake/Roast also needs 5 minutes to preheat. Then add ingredients after the 5 minutes of preheating. When cook time reaches zero, the unit will beep and "End"

Broil

Make sure the Crisper Tray is positioned elevated. After placing the ingredients in the tray, secure the lid. Then turn the Smart Switch, select the Broil mode, adjust the temperature and time and press the start button to initiate. The device will beep and show "End" when the cooking time reaches zero.

Dehydrate

Make sure the Crisper Tray is positioned at the bottom. Use the front center arrows to select Dehydrate after moving SmartSwitch to Air Fry/Stovetop. It will show the current temperature setting. The display's left side has up and down arrows that can be used to change the temperature between 105°F and 195°F. With the up and down arrows to the right of the display, you may change the cooking time in 15-minute increments between 1 and 1/2 hours. To start or stop cooking, press Start/Stop. The device will beep and show "End" when the cooking time reaches zero.

Sear/Sauté

Make sure to take the Crisper Tray out of the pot before beginning. Use the front center arrows to choose Sear/Sauté after moving SmartSwitch to Air Fry/Stovetop. To choose "Lo1," "2," "3," "4", or "Hi5", use the up and down arrows to the left of the display. To start or stop cooking, press Start/Stop. It's time to start the timer. To switch off the sear/sauté feature, press Start/Stop. Press Start/Stop to stop the cooking function, then use the center front arrow and the SmartSwitch to choose an alternative cooking function.

Sous Vide

Remove the crisper tray and fill the pot with 12 cups of room temperature water before beginning (reference the marking on the inside of the pot). Close the lid and turn the dial to "Air Fry/Stovetop" before choosing "Sous Vide" using the center arrows. It will show the current temperature setting. With the up and down arrows to the left of the display, you can select a temperature between 120°F and 190°F in 5-degree increments. By default, the cooking time will be 3 hours. The cook time can be changed using the up and down arrows to the right of the display in 15-minute intervals up to 12 hours, then in 1-hour intervals from 12 hours to 24 hours. Press START/STOP to initiate preheating.

When preheating is finished, the unit will beep, and "ADD FOOD" will appear on display. Using the water displacement method, remove the lid and drop the bags into the water: As you carefully drop the bag into the water, the pressure of the water will force the air out of the bag. Working with one bag at a time, leave a corner of the bag unzipped. Finish sealing the bag until just the seal is visible above the water line to prevent water from entering. Just above the waterline, keep the bag's seal in place.

Cleaning the Appliance

The Ninja Speedy Rapid Cooker is admired for its speedi cleanup feature as well. It has a nonstick pot for simple cleaning and a 6-quart capacity. For extra convenience, it also offers pre-set cooking programs and a delay start feature. You should first unplug the Ninja Speedi Rapid Cooker and let it cool completely before cleaning it. The nonstick pot can then be removed, washed in warm, soapy water, or put in the dishwasher. A moist cloth can also be used to clean the cooker's outside. Additionally, remove and wash the lid and the pressure release valve. Before using the cooker again, be sure to completely dry all of the components. The pressure release valve needs to be checked and cleaned on a regular basis. Water should be put through the valve to ensure that there is no food material clogging it. It's crucial to stick to the manufacturer's recommendations to avoid invalidating any warranties or harming the goods.

FAQs

1.How does the Ninja SF301 Speedi Rapid Cooker & Air Fryer work?

With its 12-in-1 features, the Ninja SF301 Speedi Rapid Cooker & Air Fryer can steam, bake, roast, sear, sauté, slow cook, sous vide, and more. The unit's lid has a Smartswitch, which makes the lid carry out cooking both through simple heating and through air frying. It employs two different heating mechanisms to cook food in different ways.

2.The Ninja SF301 Speedi Rapid Cooker & Air Fryer has a capacity of how much food?

Six quarts may be cooked in the Ninja SF301 Speedi Rapid Cooker & Air Fryer. In fact, the SF300 model also has a six-quart capacity, and it is enough to cook three parts of meals, a dinner for 4 and snacks for 6.

3.Using the Ninja SF301 Speedi Rapid Cooker & Air Fryer, how soon can I prepare a meal?

The time really depends on the type of food you are cooking. But the Ninja Speedi is more powerful, and it cooks meals quicker than traditional ovens. An entrée may be prepared using the Ninja SF301 Speedi Rapid Cooker & Air Fryer in as little as 15 minutes.

4,The Ninja SF301 Speedi Rapid Cooker & Air Fryer is what color?

Sea Salt Gray is the color of the Ninja SF301 Speedi Rapid Cooker & Air Fryer.

5.What components go into the construction of the Ninja SF301 Speedi Rapid Cooker & Air Fryer?

Stainless steel and plastic are used to construct the Ninja SF301 Speedi Rapid Cooker & Air Fryer.

Conclusion

Whether you want to pressure cook, air fry, bake, slow cook or sous vide, or more of your favorite meals, there is a dedicated recipe section for each of the cooking modes in this cookbook. The Ninja Speedi Rapid cooker is an amazing appliance, and all of its features can be best put to use when you cook a variety of snacks, entrees, desserts, and other meals for your menu. So let's get started with it.

BASIC KITCHEN CONVERSIONS & EQUIVALENTS

DRY MEASUREMENTS CONVERSION CHART

3 teaspoons = 1 tablespoon = 1/16 cup

6 teaspoons = 2 tablespoons = 1/8 cup

12 teaspoons = 4 tablespoons = ¼ cup

24 teaspoons = 8 tablespoons = ½ cup

36 teaspoons = 12 tablespoons = ¾ cup

48 teaspoons = 16 tablespoons = 1 cup

METRIC TO US COOKING CONVERSIONS

OVEN TEMPERATURES

120 ºC = 250 ºF   160 ºC = 320 ºF

180 ºC = 350 ºF   205 ºC = 400 ºF

220 ºC = 425 ºF

LIQUID MEASUREMENTS CONVERSION CHART

8 fluid ounces = 1 cup = ½ pint = ¼ quart

16 fluid ounces = 2 cups = 1 pint = ½ quart

32 fluid ounces = 4 cups = 2 pints = 1 quart = ¼ gallon

128 fluid ounces = 16 cups = 8 pints = 4 quarts = 1 gallon

BAKING IN GRAMS

1 cup flour = 140 grams

1 cup sugar = 150 grams

1 cup powdered sugar = 160 grams

1 cup heavy cream = 235 grams

VOLUME

1 milliliter = 1/5 teaspoon

5 ml = 1 teaspoon   15 ml = 1 tablespoon

240 ml = 1 cup or 8 fluid ounces

1 liter = 34 fluid ounces

WEIGHT

1 gram = .035 ounces   100 grams = 3.5 ounces

500 grams = 1.1 pounds   1 kilogram = 35 ounces

US TO METRIC COOKING CONVERSIONS

1/5 tsp = 1 ml   1 tsp = 5 ml

1 tbsp = 15 ml   1 fluid ounces = 30 ml

1 cup = 237 ml   1 pint (2 cups) = 473 ml

1 quart (4 cups) = .95 liter

1 gallon (16 cups) = 3.8 liters

1 oz = 28 grams   1 pound = 454 grams

BUTTER

1 cup butter = 2 sticks = 8 ounces = 230 grams = 16 tablespoons

WHAT DOES 1 CUP EQUAL

1 cup = 8 fluid ounces   1 cup = 16 tablespoons

1 cup = 48 teaspoons   1 cup = ½ pint

1 cup = ¼ quart   1 cup = 1/16 gallon

1 cup = 240 ml

BAKING PAN CONVERSIONS

9-inch round cake pan = 12 cups

10-inch tube pan =16 cups

10-inch bundt pan = 12 cups

9-inch springform pan = 10 cups

9 x 5 inch loaf pan = 8 cups

inch square pan = 8 cups

BAKING PAN CONVERSIONS

1 cup all-purpose flour = 4.5 oz

1 cup rolled oats = 3 oz 1 large egg = 1.7 oz

1 cup butter = 8 oz   1 cup milk = 8 oz

1 cup heavy cream = 8.4 oz

1 cup granulated sugar = 7.1 oz

1 cup packed brown sugar = 7.75 oz

1 cup vegetable oil = 7.7 oz

1 cup unsifted powdered sugar = 4.4 oz

SPEEDI MEALS

Teriyaki Salmon with Brown Rice

Prep: 12 minutes, Total Cook Time: 24 minutes, Steam: approx. 10 minutes, Cook: 14 minutes, Serves: 4

LEVEL 1 (BOTTOM OF POT)

2 tbsps. olive oil   4 cups water

2 cups easy-cooked brown rice, rinsed

Salt, to taste

LEVEL 2 (TRAY)

1 pound (454 g) salmon fillets

½ cup packed light brown sugar

½ cup rice vinegar   ½ cup soy sauce

1 tbsp. cornstarch   1 tsp. minced ginger

¼ tsp. garlic powder

TOPPINGS:

Sour cream   Tzatziki

1. Place all Level 1 ingredients in the pot and stir to combine.

2. Pull out the legs on the Crisper Tray, then place the tray in the elevated position in the pot.

3. Whisk together the remaining ingredients except the salmon fillets in a small bowl until well combined. Pour the mixture over the salmon fillets, turning to coat. Place the fillets on top of the tray.

4. Close the lid and flip the SmartSwitch to RAPID COOKER.

5. Select SPEEDI MEALS, set temperature to 350°F, and set time to 14 minutes. Press START/STOP to begin cooking (the unit will steam for approx. 10 minutes before crisping).

6. When cooking is complete, remove the salmon from the tray. Then use silicone-tipped tongs to grab the center handle and remove the tray from the unit. Transfer the rice to a bowl, then top with the salmon and toppings.

Cod and Tomato Rice Meal

Prep: 10 minutes, Total Cook Time: 22-25 minutes, Steam: approx. 10-15 minutes, Cook: 12 minutes, Serves: 2

LEVEL 1 (BOTTOM OF POT)

1 tbsp. extra virgin olive oil

1 cup white rice, rinsed and drained

2 cups water   Salt and pepper, to taste

1 large, ripe tomato, chopped

LEVEL 2 (TRAY)

2 tbsps. ghee   1 fresh large fillet cod

Salt and pepper, to taste

1. Place all Level 1 ingredients in the pot and stir to combine.

2. Pull out the legs on the Crisper Tray, then place the tray in the elevated position in the pot.

3. Cut fillet into 2 pieces. Coat with the ghee and season with salt and pepper. Place the fish on top of the tray.

4. Close the lid and flip the SmartSwitch to RAPID COOKER.

5. Select SPEEDI MEALS, set temperature to 350°F, and set time to 12 minutes. Press START/STOP to begin cooking (the unit will steam for approx. 10 to 15 minutes before crisping).

6. When cooking is complete, remove the fish from the tray. Then use silicone-tipped tongs to grab the center handle and remove the tray from the unit. Transfer the rice and tomato to a bowl, then top with the fish. Serve warm.

Tilapia Fillets with Mushroom Pasta

Prep: 5 minutes, Total Cook Time: 24 minutes, Steam: approx. 10 minutes, Cook: 14 minutes, Serves: 4

LEVEL 1 (BOTTOM OF POT)
1 tbsp. oil   ½ tsp. kosher salt
8 ounces (227 g) mushrooms, minced
½ tsp. black ground pepper
8 ounces (227 g) uncooked spaghetti pasta
2 cups water   5 ounces (142 g) spinach
½ cup pesto   ⅓ cup grated Parmesan cheese

LEVEL 2 (TRAY)
1 lemon, juiced 1 pound (454 g) tilapia fillets
½ tsp. cayenne pepper, or more to taste
2 tsps. butter, melted   ½ tsp. dried basil
Sea salt and ground black pepper, to taste
TOPPINGS:
Mustard   Salsa

1. Place all Level 1 ingredients in the pot and stir to combine.
2. Pull out the legs on the Crisper Tray, then place the tray in the elevated position in the pot.
3. Brush the fish fillets with the melted butter.
4. Sprinkle with the cayenne pepper, lemon juice, salt, and black pepper. Place the tilapia fillets on top of the tray. Sprinkle the dried basil on top.
5. Close the lid and flip the SmartSwitch to RAPID COOKER.
6. Select SPEEDI MEALS, set temperature to 350°F, and set time to 14 minutes. Press START/STOP to begin cooking (the unit will steam for approx. 10 minutes before crisping).
7. When cooking is complete, remove the tilapia fillets the tray. Then use silicone-tipped tongs to grab the center handle and remove the tray from the unit. Transfer the pasta and mushroom to a bowl, then top with the tilapia fillets and toppings.

Salmon Bok Choy Meal

Prep: 10 minutes, Total Cook Time: 24-29 minutes, Steam: approx. 10-15 minutes, Cook: 14 minutes, Serves: 4

LEVEL 1 (BOTTOM OF POT)
2 cups wild rice, soaked in water overnight and drained
4½ cups water   ½ cup raisins
2 cups Bok choy, sliced
¼ cup salted butter   1 tsp. salt

LEVEL 2 (TRAY)
2 tbsps. unsalted butter
4 (1-inch thick) salmon fillets
½ tsp. cayenne pepper ½ tsp. dried dill weed
Sea salt and freshly ground pepper, to taste
3 cloves garlic, minced 1 tsp. grated lemon zest

1. Place all Level 1 ingredients in the pot and stir to combine.
2. Pull out the legs on the Crisper Tray, then place the tray in the elevated position in the pot.
3. Brush the salmon with the melted butter and season with the cayenne pepper, salt, and black pepper on all sides. Place the salmon on top of the tray. Top with the remaining ingredients.
4. Close the lid and flip the SmartSwitch to RAPID COOKER.
5. Select SPEEDI MEALS, set temperature to 350°F, and set time to 14 minutes. Press START/STOP to begin cooking (the unit will steam for approx. 10 to 15 minutes before crisping).
6. When cooking is complete, remove the salmon from the tray. Then use silicone-tipped tongs to grab the center handle and remove the tray from the unit. Transfer the rice and Bok choy to a bowl, then top with the salmon.

Pulled Pork with Mushroom Polenta

Prep: 12 minutes, Total Cook Time: 35-40 minutes, Steam: approx. 10-15 minutes, Cook: 25 minutes, Serves: 4

LEVEL 1 (BOTTOM OF POT)

1 cup yellow cornmeal   4 cups vegetable broth

1 tbsp. butter

2 portobello mushrooms caps, finely chopped

1 tsp. onion powder   1 tsp. kosher salt

1 tsp. freshly ground black pepper

LEVEL 2 (TRAY)

1½ lbs. pork shoulder   1 tsp. cinnamon

2 tsps. garlic powder

5 tbsps. coconut oil   1 tsp. cumin powder

Salt and pepper, to taste

1. Place all Level 1 ingredients in the pot and stir to combine.
2. Pull out the legs on the Crisper Tray, then place the tray in the elevated position in the pot.
3. Mix all Level 2 ingredients in a large bowl and stir to combine well. Place the pork on top of the tray.
4. Close the lid and flip the SmartSwitch to RAPID COOKER.
5. Select SPEEDI MEALS, set temperature to 375°F, and set time to 25 minutes. Press START/STOP to begin cooking (the unit will steam for approx. 10 to 15 minutes before crisping).
6. When cooking is complete, remove the pork from the tray and and shred with two forks. Then use silicone-tipped tongs to grab the center handle and remove the tray from the unit. Transfer the Mushroom Polenta to a bowl, then top with the pork.

Ginger Pork Meatballs and Parmesan Risotto

Prep: 15 minutes, Total Cook Time: 20-25 minutes, Steam: approx. 10-15 minutes, Cook: 10 minutes, Serves: 3

LEVEL 1 (BOTTOM OF POT)

4 cups chicken broth   4 tbsps. butter

1 small onion, diced   2 garlic cloves, minced

1 cup Arborio rice   Salt and pepper, to taste

¼ cup shredded Parmesan cheese

LEVEL 2 (TRAY)

11 ounces (312 g) ground pork

1 tsp. ginger paste   1 tsp. lemon juice

¼ tsp. chili flakes

TOPPINGS:

Mustard   Sour cream

Chilli sauce

1. Place all Level 1 ingredients in the pot and stir to combine.
2. Pull out the legs on the Crisper Tray, then place the tray in the elevated position in the pot.
3. Mix the ground pork, ginger paste, lemon juice and chili flakes. Shape the mixture into small meatballs. Place the meatballs on top of the tray.
4. Close the lid and flip the SmartSwitch to RAPID COOKER.
5. Select SPEEDI MEALS, set temperature to 350°F, and set time to 10 minutes. Press START/STOP to begin cooking (the unit will steam for approx. 10 to 15 minutes before crisping).
6. When cooking is complete, remove the meatballs from the tray. Then use silicone-tipped tongs to grab the center handle and remove the tray from the unit. Transfer the Parmesan Risotto to a bowl, then top with the meatballs and toppings.

Pork and Bell Peppers with Quinoa Risotto

Prep: 18 minutes, Total Cook Time: 25-30 minutes, Steam: approx. 10-15 minutes, Cook: 15 minutes, Serves: 4

LEVEL 1 (BOTTOM OF POT)

¾ cup diced onion   1 garlic clove, minced

1 tbsp. butter   Salt and pepper, to taste

2 cups chicken broth   1 cup rinsed quinoa

¼ cup shredded Parmesan cheese

LEVEL 2 (TRAY)

2 tbsps. olive oil   4 pork chops

1 red onion, chopped

3 garlic cloves, minced

1 red bell pepper, roughly chopped

1 green bell pepper, roughly chopped

A pinch of salt and black pepper

TOPPING:

1 tbsp. parsley, chopped

1. Place all Level 1 ingredients in the pot and stir to combine.

2. Pull out the legs on the Crisper Tray, then place the tray in the elevated position in the pot.

3. Mix all Level 2 ingredients in a large bowl and stir to combine well. Place the pork mixture on top of the tray.

4. Close the lid and flip the SmartSwitch to RAPID COOKER.

5. Select SPEEDI MEALS, set temperature to 375°F, and set time to 15 minutes. Press START/STOP to begin cooking (the unit will steam for approx. 10 to 15 minutes before crisping).

6. When cooking is complete, remove the pork and bell peppers from the tray. Then use silicone-tipped tongs to grab the center handle and remove the tray from the unit. Transfer the Quinoa Risotto to a bowl, then place the pork and bell peppers on side. Serve topped with the parsley.

Chili Pork with Vegetable Quinoa

Prep: 15 minutes, Total Cook Time: 25-30 minutes, Steam: approx. 10-15 minutes, Cook: 15 minutes, Serves: 4

LEVEL 1 (BOTTOM OF POT)

1½ cups quinoa, rinsed   3 cups water

4 cups spinach   1 bell pepper, chopped

3 stalks of celery, chopped   ¼ tsp. salt

LEVEL 2 (TRAY)

4 pork chops   2 tbsps. hot sauce

2 tbsps. cocoa powder 2 tsps. chili powder

¼ tsp. ground cumin   1 tbsp. chopped parsley

A pinch of salt and black pepper

1. Place all Level 1 ingredients in the pot and stir to combine.

2. Pull out the legs on the Crisper Tray, then place the tray in the elevated position in the pot.

3. Stir all Level 2 ingredients in a large bowl and marinade for 5 minutes. Place the pork chops on top of the tray.

4. Close the lid and flip the SmartSwitch to RAPID COOKER.

5. Select SPEEDI MEALS, set temperature to 375°F, and set time to 15 minutes. Press START/STOP to begin cooking (the unit will steam for approx. 10 to 15 minutes before crisping).

6. When cooking is complete, remove the pork chops from the tray. Then use silicone-tipped tongs to grab the center handle and remove the tray from the unit. Transfer the quinoa and vegetables to a bowl, then top with the pork chops. Serve warm.

Fennel Chicken with Pea Rice

Prep: 20 minutes, Total Cook Time: 25 minutes, Steam: approx. 10 minutes, Cook: 15 minutes, Serves: 4

LEVEL 1 (BOTTOM OF POT)

1 tbsp. olive oil   1 clove garlic, minced

¼ cup chopped shallots

2 cups chicken broth

1 cup basmati rice, rinsed

1 cup frozen peas

½ cup chopped carrots

2 tsps. curry powder

Salt and ground black pepper, to taste

LEVEL 2 (TRAY)

3 tbsps. freshly squeezed lemon juice

1 tsp. cinnamon   ¼ cup fennel bulb

4 garlic cloves, minced

4 (5-6 oz each) boneless and skinless chicken thighs

Salt and pepper, to taste

TOPPINGS:

Sesame seeds   Tzatziki

1. Place all Level 1 ingredients in the pot and stir to combine.
2. Pull out the legs on the Crisper Tray, then place the tray in the elevated position in the pot.
3. Mix all Level 2 ingredients in a large bowl and marinade for 5 minutes. Place the chicken mixture on top of the tray.
4. Close the lid and flip the SmartSwitch to RAPID COOKER.
5. Select SPEEDI MEALS, set temperature to 390°F, and set time to 15 minutes. Press START/STOP to begin cooking (the unit will steam for approx. 10 minutes before crisping).
6. When cooking is complete, remove the chicken from the tray. Then use silicone-tipped tongs to grab the center handle and remove the tray from the unit. Transfer the pea rice to a bowl, then top with the chicken and toppings.

Chicken Drumsticks with Chickpea Rice

Prep: 20 minutes, Total Cook Time: 30-35 minutes, Steam: approx. 10-15 minutes, Cook: 20 minutes, Serves: 4

LEVEL 1 (BOTTOM OF POT)

½ cup canned chickpeas   4½ cups water

1 cup deseeded and minced ripe tomato

Salt and pepper, to taste

1½ cups rinsed and drained white rice

LEVEL 2 (TRAY)

¼ tsp. dried thyme   1½ tbsps. paprika

Salt and pepper, to taste

½ tsp. onion powder

4 (5-6 oz each) chicken drumsticks

1. Place all Level 1 ingredients in the pot and stir to combine.
2. Pull out the legs on the Crisper Tray, then place the tray in the elevated position in the pot.
3. On a clean work surface, rub the chicken drumsticks generously with the spices. Season with salt and pepper. Place the chicken on top of the tray.
4. Close the lid and flip the SmartSwitch to RAPID COOKER.
5. Select SPEEDI MEALS, set temperature to 390°F, and set time to 20 minutes. Press START/STOP to begin cooking (the unit will steam for approx. 10 to 15 minutes before crisping).
6. When cooking is complete, remove the chicken from the tray. Then use silicone-tipped tongs to grab the center handle and remove the tray from the unit. Transfer the Chickpea Rice to a bowl, then top with the chicken. Serve warm.

Jamaican Chicken Drumsticks with Couscous

Prep: 15 minutes, Total Cook Time: 30-35 minutes, Steam: approx. 10-15 minutes, Cook: 20 minutes, Serves: 4

LEVEL 1 (BOTTOM OF POT)

1 tbsp. butter	1 cup couscous
2½ cups vegetable broth	
½ cup chopped spinach, blanched	
1½ tomatoes, chopped	

LEVEL 2 (TRAY)

4 (5-6 oz each) chicken drumsticks	
1 tbsp. Jamaican curry powder	
1 tsp. salt	½ medium onion, diced
½ tsp. dried thyme	

1. Place all Level 1 ingredients in the pot and stir to combine.
2. Pull out the legs on the Crisper Tray, then place the tray in the elevated position in the pot.
3. Sprinkle the salt and curry powder over the chicken drumsticks. Place the chicken on top of the tray, along with the remaining ingredients.
4. Close the lid and flip the SmartSwitch to RAPID COOKER.
5. Select SPEEDI MEALS, set temperature to 390°F, and set time to 20 minutes. Press START/STOP to begin cooking (the unit will steam for approx. 10 to 15 minutes before crisping).
6. When cooking is complete, remove the chicken from the tray. Then use silicone-tipped tongs to grab the center handle and remove the tray from the unit. Transfer the couscous and vegetables to a bowl, then top with the chicken.
7. Serve warm.

Crispy Wings with Broccoli Pasta

Prep: 25 minutes, Total Cook Time: 30 minutes, Steam: approx. 10 minutes, Cook: 20 minutes, Serves: 4

LEVEL 1 (BOTTOM OF POT)

2 cups water	½ pound (227 g) pasta
½ cup broccoli	½ cup half and half
8 ounces (227 g) grated Cheddar cheese	
Salt, to taste	

LEVEL 2 (TRAY)

1 tbsp. paprika	1 tsp. rosemary leaves
Salt and pepper, to taste	4 chicken wings
TOPPINGS:	
Tzatziki	Chilli sauce

1. Place all Level 1 ingredients in the pot and stir to combine.
2. Pull out the legs on the Crisper Tray, then place the tray in the elevated position in the pot.
3. Season the chicken wings on all sides with paprika, rosemary, salt, and pepper. Place the chicken wings on top of the tray.
4. Close the lid and flip the SmartSwitch to RAPID COOKER.
5. Select SPEEDI MEALS, set temperature to 450°F, and set time to 20 minutes. Press START/STOP to begin cooking (the unit will steam for approx. 10 minutes before crisping).
6. When cooking is complete, remove the chicken wings from the tray. Then use silicone-tipped tongs to grab the center handle and remove the tray from the unit. Transfer the Broccoli Pasta to a bowl, then top with the chicken wings and toppings.

Herbed Sirloin Tip Roast and Tomato Pasta

Prep: 25 minutes, Total Cook Time: 28 minutes, Steam: approx. 10 minutes, Cook: 18 minutes, Serves: 6

LEVEL 1 (BOTTOM OF POT)

2 cups dried campanelle pasta

6 cups vegetable stock   ½ tsp. salt

2 tomatoes, cut into large dices

1 or 2 pinches red pepper flakes

½ tsp. dried oregano   ½ tsp. garlic powder

10 to 12 fresh sweet basil leaves, finely chopped

Freshly ground black pepper, to taste

LEVEL 2 (TRAY)

2 tbsps. mixed herbs   1 tsp. garlic powder

2 lbs. sirloin tip roast   1¼ tsps. paprika

Salt and pepper, to taste

1. Place all Level 1 ingredients in the pot and stir to combine.
2. Pull out the legs on the Crisper Tray, then place the tray in the elevated position in the pot.
3. Mix the roast with all the remaining ingredients. Place the roast on top of the tray.
4. Close the lid and flip the SmartSwitch to RAPID COOKER.
5. Select SPEEDI MEALS, set temperature to 360°F, and set time to 18 minutes. Press START/STOP to begin cooking (the unit will steam for approx. 10 minutes before crisping).
6. When cooking is complete, remove the roast from the tray and shred with two forks. Then use silicone-tipped tongs to grab the center handle and remove the tray from the unit. Transfer the pasta and tomato to a bowl, then top with the roast. Serve warm.

Beef Steak and Mushroom Alfredo Rice

Prep: 20 minutes, Total Cook Time: 25 minutes, Steam: approx. 10 minutes, Cook: 15 minutes, Serves: 4

LEVEL 1 (BOTTOM OF POT)

2 tbsps. olive oil

¾ cup finely chopped onion

2 garlic cloves, minced   1 cup rice

2½ cups vegetable broth

1½ tbsps. fresh lemon juice

Salt and black pepper, to taste

2 ounces (57 g) creamy mushroom Alfredo sauce

¼ cup coarsely chopped walnuts

LEVEL 2 (TRAY)

½ cup butter, melted   1 tsp. ground nutmeg

1 pound (454 g) beef steak   ½ tsp. salt

1. Place all Level 1 ingredients in the pot and stir to combine.
2. Pull out the legs on the Crisper Tray, then place the tray in the elevated position in the pot.
3. Mix the beef steaks on all sides with melted butter, nutmeg, and salt. Then place the steaks on top of the tray.
4. Close the lid and flip the SmartSwitch to RAPID COOKER.
5. Select SPEEDI MEALS, set temperature to 350°F, and set time to 15 minutes. Press START/STOP to begin cooking (the unit will steam for approx. 10 minutes before crisping).
6. When cooking is complete, remove the steaks from the tray. Then use silicone-tipped tongs to grab the center handle and remove the tray from the unit. Transfer the Mushroom Alfredo Rice to a bowl, then top with the steaks.
7. Serve warm.

Beef Meatballs and Tomato Meal

Prep: 15 minutes, Total Cook Time: 20-25 minutes, Steam: approx. 10-15 minutes, Cook: 10 minutes, Serves: 4

LEVEL 1 (BOTTOM OF POT)

¾ cup (or more) short grain brown rice, rinsed

3 to 4 tbsps. red, wild or black rice, rinsed

1½ cups water   ¼ tsp. sea salt

LEVEL 2 (TRAY)

1 lb. lean ground beef   2 large eggs

3 tbsps. all-purpose flour

Salt and pepper, to taste

2 cups diced tomatoes

1. Place all Level 1 ingredients in the pot and stir to combine.

2. Pull out the legs on the Crisper Tray, then place the tray in the elevated position in the pot.

3. In a large bowl, thoroughly mix the beef, eggs, and flour, then sprinkle with salt and pepper. Mix well and make 6 meatballs of 1½ inch. Place the meatballs on top of the tray. Top with the tomatoes.

4. Close the lid and flip the SmartSwitch to RAPID COOKER.

5. Select SPEEDI MEALS, set temperature to 350°F, and set time to 10 minutes. Press START/STOP to begin cooking (the unit will steam for approx. 10 to 15 minutes before crisping).

6. When cooking is complete, remove the meatballs and tomato from the tray. Then use silicone-tipped tongs to grab the center handle and remove the tray from the unit. Transfer the rice to a bowl, then top with the meatballs and tomato.

Cheese Stuffed Mushrooms

Prep: 15 minutes, Total Cook Time: 20 minutes, Steam: approx. 4 minutes, Cook: 16 minutes, Serves: 4

½ cup water, for steaming

4 fresh large mushrooms, stemmed and gills removed

¼ cup Parmesan cheese, shredded

2 tbsps. white cheddar cheese, shredded

2 tbsps. sharp cheddar cheese, shredded

Salt and black pepper, to taste

⅓ cup vegetable oil

4 ounces cream cheese, softened

1 tsp. Worcestershire sauce

2 garlic cloves, chopped

Salt and ground black pepper, as required

1. Pour ½ cup water into the pot. Push in the legs on the Crisper Tray, then place the tray in the bottom position in the pot.

2. Mix together Parmesan cheese, cheddar cheese, Worcestershire sauce, cream cheese, garlic, salt and black pepper in a bowl,

3. Stuff the cheese mixture in each mushroom and arrange on the tray.

4. Close the lid and flip the SmartSwitch to Rapid Cooker. Select STEAM & CRISP, set temperature to 375°F, and set time to 16 minutes. Press START/STOP to begin cooking (the unit will steam for approx. 4 minutes before crisping).

5. When cooking is complete, dish out in a serving platter.

Chicken Nuggets

Prep: 15 minutes, Total Cook Time: 19 minutes, Steam: approx. 4 minutes, Cook: 15 minutes, Serves: 4

½ cup water, for steaming
20-ounce chicken breast, cut into chunks
1 cup all-purpose flour   2 tbsps. milk
1 egg   1 cup panko breadcrumbs

½ tbsp. mustard powder
1 tbsp. garlic powder   1 tbsp. onion powder
Salt and black pepper, to taste

1. Pour ½ cup water into the pot. Pull out the legs on the Crisper Tray, then place the tray in the elevated position in the pot.
2. Put chicken along with mustard powder, garlic powder, onion powder, salt and black pepper in a food processor and pulse until combined.
3. Place flour in a shallow dish and whisk the eggs with milk in a second dish.
4. Place breadcrumbs in a third shallow dish.
5. Coat the nuggets evenly in flour and dip in the egg mixture.
6. Roll into the breadcrumbs evenly and arrange the nuggets on the tray.
7. Close the lid and flip the SmartSwitch to Rapid Cooker. Select STEAM & CRISP, set temperature to 375°F, and set time to 15 minutes. Press START/STOP to begin cooking (the unit will steam for approx. 4 minutes before crisping).
8. With 7 minutes remaining, open the lid and flip once. Close the lid to continue cooking.
9. When cooking is complete, serve hot.

Vegetable Nuggets

Prep: 15 minutes, Total Cook Time: 19 minutes, Steam: approx. 4 minutes, Cook: 15 minutes, Serves: 4

½ cup water, for steaming
1 zucchini, chopped roughly
½ of carrot, chopped roughly
1 cup all-purpose flour

1 egg   1 cup panko breadcrumbs
1 tbsp. garlic powder   ½ tbsp. mustard powder
1 tbsp. onion powder
Salt and black pepper, to taste

1. Pour ½ cup water into the pot. Push in the legs on the Crisper Tray, then place the tray in the bottom position in the pot.
2. Put zucchini, carrot, mustard powder, garlic powder, onion powder, salt and black pepper in a food processor and pulse until combined.
3. Place flour in a shallow dish and whisk the eggs with milk in a second dish.
4. Place breadcrumbs in a third shallow dish.
5. Coat the vegetable nuggets evenly in flour and dip in the egg mixture.
6. Roll into the breadcrumbs evenly and arrange the nuggets on the tray.
7. Close the lid and flip the SmartSwitch to Rapid Cooker. Select STEAM & CRISP, set temperature to 350°F, and set time to 15 minutes. Press START/STOP to begin cooking (the unit will steam for approx. 4 minutes before crisping).
8. With 8 minutes remaining, open the lid and flip the nuggets with tongs. Close the lid to continue cooking.
9. When cooking is complete, dish out to serve warm.

Italian Beef Meatballs

Prep: 10 minutes, Total Cook Time: 17 minutes, Steam: approx. 4 minutes, Cook: 13 minutes, Serves: 6

½ cup water, for steaming 　　 2 large eggs 　　 ¼ cup Parmigiano Reggiano, grated
2 pounds ground beef 　　　　　 1 tsp. dried oregano 　　 1 tsp. vegetable oil
¼ cup fresh parsley, chopped 　　 1 small garlic clove, chopped
1¼ cups panko breadcrumbs 　　 Salt and black pepper, to taste

1. Pour ½ cup water into the pot. Push in the legs on the Crisper Tray, then place the tray in the bottom position in the pot.
2. Mix beef with all other ingredients in a bowl until well combined.
3. Make equal-sized balls from the mixture and arrange the balls on the tray.
4. Close the lid and flip the SmartSwitch to Rapid Cooker. Select STEAM & CRISP, set temperature to 350°F, and set time to 13 minutes. Press START/STOP to begin cooking (the unit will steam for approx. 4 minutes before crisping).
5. With 6 minutes remaining, open the lid and flip the side with tongs. Close the lid to continue cooking.
6. When cooking is complete, serve warm.

Spicy Jacket Potatoes

Prep: 15 minutes, Total Cook Time: 40 minutes, Steam: approx. 10 minutes, Cook: 30 minutes, Serves: 2

1 cup water, for steaming 　　 2 potatoes 　　 ¼ cup tomatoes, chopped
1 tbsp. parmesan cheese, shredded 　　 3 tbsps. sour cream
1 tbsp. butter, softened 　 1 tsp. parsley, minced 　　 Salt and black pepper, to taste

1. Pour 1 cup water into the pot. Push in the legs on the Crisper Tray, then place the tray in the bottom position in the pot.
2. Make holes in the potatoes and transfer to the tray.
3. Close the lid and flip the SmartSwitch to Rapid Cooker. Select STEAM & CRISP, set temperature to 400°F, and set time to 30 minutes. Press START/STOP to begin cooking (the unit will steam for approx. 10 minutes before crisping).
4. When cooking is complete, transfer the potatoes in a bowl.
5. Mix together rest of the ingredients in another bowl and combine well.
6. Cut the potatoes from the center and stuff in the cheese mixture to serve.

Buttered Corn on the Cob

Prep: 10 minutes, Total Cook Time: 28 minutes, Steam: approx. 8 minutes, Cook: 20 minutes, Serves: 2

½ cup water, for steaming 　　 2 corns on the cob 　　 Salt and black pepper, to taste
2 tbsps. butter, softened and divided

1. Pour ½ cup water into the pot. Push in the legs on the Crisper Tray, then place the tray in the bottom position in the pot.
2. Season the cobs evenly with salt and black pepper and rub with 1 tbsp. butter.
3. Wrap the cobs in foil paper and arrange on the tray.
4. Close the lid and flip the SmartSwitch to Rapid Cooker. Select STEAM & CRISP, set temperature to 320°F, and set time to 20 minutes. Press START/STOP to begin cooking (the unit will steam for approx. 8 minutes before crisping).
5. When cooking is complete, top with remaining butter. Serve warm.

Rice Flour Crusted Tofu

Prep: 15 minutes, Total Cook Time: 18-19 minutes, Steam: approx. 3-4 minutes, Cook: 15 minutes, Serves: 3

½ cup water, for steaming   2 tbsps. olive oil   2 tbsps. cornstarch   ¼ cup rice flour

1 (14-ounces) block firm tofu, pressed and cubed into ½-inch size   Salt and ground black pepper, as required

1. Pour ½ cup water into the pot. Push in the legs on the Crisper Tray, then place the tray in the bottom position in the pot.
2. Mix together cornstarch, rice flour, salt, and black pepper in a bowl.
3. Coat the tofu with flour mixture evenly and drizzle with olive oil.
4. Arrange the tofu cubes on the tray.
5. Close the lid and flip the SmartSwitch to Rapid Cooker. Select STEAM & CRISP, set temperature to 390°F, and set time to 15 minutes. Press START/STOP to begin cooking (the unit will steam for approx. 3 to 4 minutes before crisping).
6. With 8 minutes remaining, open the lid and toss the tofu cubes with tongs. Close the lid to continue cooking.
7. When cooking is complete, transfer the tofu into a serving platter and serve warm.

Spicy Broccoli Poppers

Prep: 25 minutes, Total Cook Time: 14 minutes, Steam: approx. 4 minutes, Cook: 10 minutes, Serves: 4

½ cup water, for steaming   2 tbsps. chickpea flour   ½ tsp. red chili powder

2 tbsps. plain yogurt   ¼ tsp. ground cumin   ¼ tsp. ground turmeric

1 pound broccoli, cut into small florets   Salt, to taste

1. Pour ½ cup water into the pot. Push in the legs on the Crisper Tray, then place the tray in the bottom position in the pot.
2. Mix together the yogurt, red chili powder, cumin, turmeric and salt in a bowl until well combined.
3. Stir in the broccoli and generously coat with marinade.
4. Refrigerate for about 30 minutes and sprinkle the broccoli florets with chickpea flour.
5. Arrange the broccoli florets on the tray.
6. Close the lid and flip the SmartSwitch to Rapid Cooker. Select STEAM & CRISP, set temperature to 400°F, and set time to 10 minutes. Press START/STOP to begin cooking (the unit will steam for approx. 4 minutes before crisping).
7. With 5 minutes remaining, open the lid and toss the broccoli florets with tongs. Close the lid to continue cooking.
8. When cooking is complete, serve warm.

Bacon-Wrapped Shrimp

Prep: 15 minutes, Total Cook Time: 12 minutes, Steam: approx. 4 minutes, Cook: 8 minutes, Serves: 6

½ cup water, for steaming
1 pound bacon, sliced thinly

1 pound shrimp, peeled and deveined
Salt, to taste

1. Pour ½ cup water into the pot. Push in the legs on the Crisper Tray, then place the tray in the bottom position in the pot.
2. Wrap shrimp with salt and a bacon slices, covering completely.
3. Repeat with the remaining shrimp and bacon slices.
4. Arrange the bacon wrapped shrimps in a baking dish and freeze for about 15 minutes.
5. Place the shrimps on the tray.
6. Close the lid and flip the SmartSwitch to Rapid Cooker. Select STEAM & CRISP, set temperature to 375°F, and set time to 8 minutes. Press START/STOP to begin cooking (the unit will steam for approx. 4 minutes before crisping).
7. When the time is up, dish out and serve warm.

Delightful Fish Nuggets

Prep: 15 minutes, Total Cook Time: 14 minutes, Steam: approx. 4 minutes, Cook: 10 minutes, Serves: 4

½ cup water, for steaming
1 cup all-purpose flou
¾ cup breadcrumbs

2 eggs

1 pound cod, cut into 1x2½-inch strips
Pinch of salt
2 tbsps. olive oil

1. Pour ½ cup water into the pot. Pull out the legs on the Crisper Tray, then place the tray in the elevated position in the pot.
2. Place flour in a shallow dish and whisk the eggs in a second dish.
3. Mix breadcrumbs, salt and oil in a third shallow dish.
4. Coat the fish strips evenly in flour and dip in the egg.
5. Roll into the breadcrumbs evenly and arrange the nuggets on the tray.
6. Close the lid and flip the SmartSwitch to Rapid Cooker. Select STEAM & CRISP, set temperature to 400°F, and set time to 10 minutes. Press START/STOP to begin cooking (the unit will steam for approx. 4 minutes before crisping).
7. With 5 minutes remaining, open the lid and flip the nuggets with tongs. Close the lid to continue cooking.
8. When cooking is complete, dish out to serve warm.

Stuffed Mushrooms with Sour Cream

Prep: 10 minutes, Total Cook Time: 21 minutes, Steam: approx. 4 minutes, Cook: 17 minutes, Makes: 12 mushroom caps

½ cup water, for steaming
¼ orange bell pepper, diced
¾ cup Cheddar cheese, shredded
12 mushroom caps, stems diced   ½ onion,

diced
½ small carrot, diced   ¼ cup sour cream

1. Pour ½ cup water into the pot. Push in the legs on the Crisper Tray, then place the tray in the bottom position in the pot.
2. Place mushroom stems, onion, orange bell pepper and carrot over medium heat in a skillet.
3. Cook for about 5 minutes until softened and stir in ½ cup Cheddar cheese and sour cream.
4. Stuff this mixture in the mushroom caps and arrange them on the tray. Top with rest of the cheese.
5. Close the lid and flip the SmartSwitch to Rapid Cooker. Select STEAM & CRISP, set temperature to 350°F, and set time to 12 minutes. Press START/STOP to begin cooking (the unit will steam for approx. 4 minutes before crisping), until cheese is melted.
6. Serve warm.

Basic Salmon Croquettes

Prep: 15 minutes, Total Cook Time: 12 minutes, Steam: approx. 4 minutes, Cook: 8 minutes, Makes: 16 croquettes

½ cup water, for steaming

2 eggs, lightly beaten

1 large can red salmon, drained

2 tbsps. fresh parsley, chopped

1 cup breadcrumbs   2 tbsps. milk

Salt and black pepper, to taste

⅓ cup vegetable oil

1. Pour ½ cup water into the pot. Pull out the legs on the Crisper Tray, then place the tray in the elevated position in the pot.

2. Mash the salmon completely in a bowl and stir in eggs, parsley, breadcrumbs, milk, salt and black pepper.

3. Mix until well combined and make 16 equal-sized croquettes from the mixture.

4. Mix together oil and breadcrumbs in a shallow dish and coat the croquettes in this mixture.

5. Place the croquettes on the tray.

6. Close the lid and flip the SmartSwitch to Rapid Cooker. Select STEAM & CRISP, set temperature to 400°F, and set time to 8 minutes. Press START/STOP to begin cooking (the unit will steam for approx. 4 minutes before crisping).

7. With 4 minutes remaining, open the lid and flip the croquettes with tongs. Close the lid to continue cooking.

8. When cooking is complete, transfer into a serving bowl and serve warm.

Bacon Filled Poppers

Prep: 5 minutes, Total Cook Time: 22 minutes, Steam: approx. 4 minutes, Cook: 18 minutes, Serves: 4

½ cup water, for steaming

4 strips crispy cooked bacon

3 tbsps. butter   ⅔ cup almond flour

½ cup jalapeno peppers, diced

2 oz. Cheddar cheese, white, shredded

1 pinch cayenne pepper   1 tbsp. bacon fat

1 tsp. kosher salt

Black pepper, ground, to taste

1. Pour ½ cup water into the pot. Push in the legs on the Crisper Tray, then place the tray in the bottom position in the pot.

2. Mix together butter with salt and water on medium heat in a skillet.

3. Whisk in the flour and sauté for about 3 minutes.

4. Dish out in a bowl and mix with the remaining ingredients to form a dough.

5. Wrap plastic wrap around the dough and refrigerate for about half an hour.

6. Make small popper balls out of this dough and arrange on the tray.

7. Close the lid and flip the SmartSwitch to Rapid Cooker. Select STEAM & CRISP, set temperature to 390°F, and set time to 15 minutes. Press START/STOP to begin cooking (the unit will steam for approx. 4 minutes before crisping).

8. With 7 minutes remaining, open the lid and flip the balls with tongs. Close the lid to continue cooking.

9. When cooking is complete, dish out to serve warm.

Nutty Cauliflower Poppers

Prep: 10 minutes, Total Cook Time: 24 minutes, Steam: approx. 4 minutes, Cook: 20 minutes, Serves: 4

½ cup water, for steaming

1 cup boiling water, for soaking the raisins

¼ cup golden raisins   ¼ cup toasted pine nuts

¼ tsp. salt

1 head of cauliflower, cut into small florets

½ cup olive oil   1 tbsp. curry powder

1. Pour ½ cup water into the pot. Push in the legs on the Crisper Tray, then place the tray in the bottom position in the pot.
2. Put raisins in boiling water in a bowl and keep aside.
3. Mix together cauliflower, pine nuts, salt, curry powder and olive oil in a large bowl.
4. Transfer this mixture on the tray.
5. Close the lid and flip the SmartSwitch to Rapid Cooker. Select STEAM & CRISP, set temperature to 425°F, and set time to 20 minutes. Press START/STOP to begin cooking (the unit will steam for approx. 4 minutes before crisping).
6. With 10 minutes remaining, open the lid and toss the cauliflower with tongs. Close the lid to continue cooking.
7. When cooking is complete, dish out the cauliflower in a serving bowl.
8. Drain raisins and add to the serving bowl.

Ranch Dipped Fillets

Prep: 5 minutes, Total Cook Time: 13 minutes, Steam: approx. 4 minutes, Cook: 9 minutes, Serves: 2

½ cup water, for steaming

¼ cup panko breadcrumbs

½ packet ranch dressing mix powder

2 tilapia fillets

1 egg beaten

1¼ tbsps. vegetable oil

FOR GARNISH:

Herbs and chilies

1. Pour ½ cup water into the pot. Pull out the legs on the Crisper Tray, then place the tray in the elevated position in the pot.
2. Mix ranch dressing with panko breadcrumbs in a bowl.
3. Whisk eggs in a shallow bowl and dip the fish fillet in the eggs.
4. Dredge in the breadcrumbs and transfer on the tray.
5. Close the lid and flip the SmartSwitch to Rapid Cooker. Select STEAM & CRISP, set temperature to 450°F, and set time to 9 minutes. Press START/STOP to begin cooking (the unit will steam for approx. 4 minutes before crisping).
6. With 4 minutes remaining, open the lid and flip the fillets with tongs. Close the lid to continue cooking.
7. When cooking is complete, transfer the fillets to two serving bowls. Garnish with chilies and herbs to serve.

STEAM&BAKE

Citric Chocolate Pudding

Prep: 10 minutes, Total Cook Time: 34 minutes, Steam: approx. 20 minutes, Cook: 14 minutes, Serves: 4

2 cups water, for steaming   cooking spray   2 tsps. fresh orange rind, grated finely

½ cup butter   2 medium eggs   2 tbsps. self-rising flour ¼ cup caster sugar

⅔ cup dark chocolate, chopped   ¼ cup fresh orange juice

1. Pour 2 cups water into the pot. Push in the legs on the Crisper Tray, then place the tray in the bottom position in the pot. Spray 4 ramekins with cooking spray.

2. Microwave butter and chocolate in a bowl on high for about 2 minutes.

3. Add sugar, eggs, orange rind and juice and mix until well combined.

4. Stir in the flour and mix well.

5. Divide this mixture into the ramekins. Transfer the ramekins to the prepared pan, then place the pan on the tray.

6. Close the lid and flip the SmartSwitch to Rapid Cooker. Select STEAM & BAKE, set temperature to 350°F, and set time to 12 minutes. Press START/STOP to begin cooking (the unit will steam for approx. 20 minutes before baking).

7. Dish out and serve chilled.

Heavenly Tasty Lava Cake

Prep: 10 minutes, Total Cook Time: 25 minutes, Steam: approx. 20 minutes, Cook: 5 minutes, Serves: 6

2 cups water, for steaming   cooking spray

⅔ cup unsalted butter   2 eggs

⅔ cup all-purpose flour ⅓ cup fresh raspberries

1 cup chocolate chips, melted

5 tbsps. sugar   Salt, to taste

1. Pour 2 cups water into the pot. Push in the legs on the Crisper Tray, then place the tray in the bottom position in the pot. Spray 6 ramekins with cooking spray.

2. Mix sugar, butter, eggs, chocolate mixture, flour and salt in a bowl until well combined.

3. Fold in the melted chocolate chips and divide this mixture into the prepared ramekins. Transfer the ramekins on the tray.

4. Close the lid and flip the SmartSwitch to Rapid Cooker. Select STEAM & BAKE, set temperature to 300°F, and set time to 5 minutes. Press START/STOP to begin cooking (the unit will steam for approx. 20 minutes before baking).

5. Garnish with raspberries and serve immediately.

Beef Pot Pie

Prep: 10 minutes, Total Cook Time: 1 hour 41 minutes, Steam: approx. 20 minutes, Cook: 1 hour 21 minutes, Serves: 3

1 cup water, for steaming   cooking spray   1 prepared short crust pastry   1 tbsp. olive oil

1 pound beef stewing steak, cubed   1 tbsp. tomato puree   2 tbsps. onion paste

1 can ale mixed into 1 cup water   Salt and black pepper, to taste

2 beef bouillon cubes   1 tbsp. plain flour

1. Pour 1 cup water into the pot. Push in the legs on the Crisper Tray, then place the tray in the bottom position in the pot. Spray 2 ramekins with cooking spray.

2. Heat olive oil in a pan and add steak cubes.

3. Cook for about 5 minutes and stir in the onion paste and tomato puree.

4. Cook for about 6 minutes and add the ale mixture, bouillon cubes, salt and black pepper.

5. Bring to a boil and reduce the heat to simmer for about 1 hour.

6. Mix flour and 3 tbsps. of warm water in a bowl and slowly add this mixture into the beef mixture.

7. Roll out the short crust pastry and line 2 ramekins with pastry.

8. Divide the beef mixture evenly in the ramekins and top with extra pastry. Transfer the ramekins on the tray.

9. Close the lid and flip the SmartSwitch to Rapid Cooker. Select STEAM & BAKE, set temperature to 350°F, and set time to 10 minutes. Press START/STOP to begin cooking (the unit will steam for approx. 20 minutes before baking).

10. When cooking is complete, dish out and serve warm.

11. Dish out and serve warm.

Beef and Mushroom Meatloaf

Prep: 15 minutes, Total Cook Time: 38 minutes, Steam: approx. 20 minutes, Cook: 18 minutes, Serves: 4

1 cup water, for steaming   cooking spray   beaten

1 pound lean ground beef   1 tbsp. olive oil   2 mushrooms, thickly sliced

1 small onion, finely chopped   Salt and ground black pepper, as required

3 tbsps. dry breadcrumbs   1   egg,   lightly

1. Pour 1 cup water into the pot. Push in the legs on the Crisper Tray, then place the tray in the bottom position in the pot. Spray a 8-inch round baking pan with cooking spray.

2. Mix the beef, onion, olive oil, breadcrumbs, egg, salt, and black pepper in a bowl until well combined.

3. Shape the mixture into loaves and top with mushroom slices.

4. Arrange the loaves in the prepared pan, then place the pan on the tray.

5. Close the lid and flip the SmartSwitch to Rapid Cooker. Select STEAM & BAKE, set temperature to 350°F, and set time to 18 minutes. Press START/STOP to begin cooking (the unit will steam for approx. 20 minutes before baking).

6. Cut into desired size wedges and serve warm.

Walnut Banana Cake

Prep: 5 minutes, Total Cook Time: 40 minutes, Steam: approx. 20 minutes, Cook: 20 minutes, Serves: 6

2 cups water, for steaming   cooking spray   ½ tsp. ground cinnamon   Salt, to taste
1½ cups cake flour   1 tsp. baking soda   ½ cup vegetable oil   ½ tsp. vanilla
2 eggs   3 medium bananas, peeled and mashed   extract
½ cup walnuts, chopped   ½ cup sugar

1. Pour 2 cups water into the pot. Push in the legs on the Crisper Tray, then place the tray in the bottom position in the pot. Spray a 8-inch round baking pan with cooking spray.

2. Mix flour, baking soda, cinnamon and salt in a bowl until well combined.

3. Whisk egg with oil, vanilla extract, sugar and bananas in another bowl.

4. Stir in the flour mixture slowly and fold in the apples.

5. Pour this mixture into the baking pan and top with walnuts and raisins.

6. Cover with the foil paper and transfer the baking pan on the tray.

7. Close the lid and flip the SmartSwitch to Rapid Cooker. Select STEAM & BAKE, set temperature to 315°F, and set time to 20 minutes. Press START/STOP to begin cooking (the unit will steam for approx. 20 minutes before baking).

8. With 5 minutes remaining, open the lid and remove the foil. Close the lid to continue cooking.

9. When the time is up, cut the cake into slices to serve.

Chocolate Lover's Muffins

Prep: 10 minutes, Total Cook Time: 25 minutes, Steam: approx. 15 minutes, Cook: 10 minutes, Serves: 8

1 cup water, for steaming   cooking spray   1 cup yogurt   ¼ cup sugar
1½ cups all-purpose flour   2 tsps. baking   Salt, to taste   ⅓ cup vegetable oil
powder   2 tsps. vanilla extract
½ cup mini chocolate chips   1 egg

1. Pour 1 cup water into the pot. Push in the legs on the Crisper Tray, then place the tray in the bottom position in the pot. Spray 8 muffin cups with cooking spray.

2. Mix flour, baking powder, sugar and salt in a bowl.

3. Whisk egg, oil, yogurt and vanilla extract in another bowl.

4. Combine the flour and egg mixtures and mix until a smooth mixture is formed.

5. Fold in the chocolate chips and divide this mixture into the prepared muffin cups.

6. Transfer the muffin cups on the tray.

7. Close the lid and flip the SmartSwitch to Rapid Cooker. Select STEAM & BAKE, set temperature to 350°F, and set time to 10 minutes. Press START/STOP to begin cooking (the unit will steam for approx. 15 minutes before baking).

8. Refrigerate for 2 hours and serve chilled.

Simple Beef Burgers

Prep: 20 minutes, Total Cook Time: 44 minutes, Steam: approx. 20 minutes, Cook: 24 minutes, Serves: 6

1 cup water, for steaming
2 pounds ground beef
12 cheddar cheese slices   12 dinner rolls

6 tbsps. tomato ketchup
Salt and black pepper, to taste

1. Pour 1 cup water into the pot. Push in the legs on the Crisper Tray, then place the tray in the bottom position in the pot. Spray a 8-inch round baking pan with cooking spray.
2. Mix the beef, salt and black pepper in a bowl.
3. Make small equal-sized patties from the beef mixture and arrange half of patties to the prepared pan, then place the pan on the tray.
4. Close the lid and flip the SmartSwitch to Rapid Cooker. Select STEAM & BAKE, set temperature to 375°F, and set time to 12 minutes. Press START/STOP to begin cooking (the unit will steam for approx. 10 minutes before baking).
5. Arrange the patties between rolls and drizzle with ketchup.
6. Repeat with the remaining batch and dish out to serve hot.

Red Velvet Cupcakes

Prep: 15 minutes, Total Cook Time: 32 minutes, Steam: approx. 20 minutes, Cook: 12 minutes, Serves: 12

1 cup water, for steaming   cooking spray
FOR CUPCAKES:
2 cups refined flour   ¾ cup peanut butter
3 eggs   ¾ cup icing sugar
2 tsps. beet powder   1 tsp. cocoa powder

FOR FROSTING:
1 cup butter   1 cup cream cheese
¾ cup icing sugar   ¼ cup strawberry sauce
1 tsp. vanilla essence

1. Pour 1 cup water into the pot. Push in the legs on the Crisper Tray, then place the tray in the bottom position in the pot. Spray 12 silicon cups with cooking spray.
2. Mix all the Cupcakes ingredients in a large bowl until well combined.
3. Transfer the mixture into silicon cups and place on the tray.
4. Close the lid and flip the SmartSwitch to Rapid Cooker. Select STEAM & BAKE, set temperature to 350°F, and set time to 12 minutes. Press START/STOP to begin cooking (the unit will steam for approx. 20 minutes before baking).
5. Mix all the Frosting ingredients in a large bowl until well combined.
6. Top each cupcake evenly with frosting and serve.

Cheesy Dinner Rolls

Prep: 10 minutes, Total Cook Time: 12 minutes, Steam: approx. 4 minutes, Cook: 8 minutes, Serves: 2

1 cup water, for steaming   cooking spray
2 dinner rolls   ½ cup Parmesan cheese, grated

2 tbsps. unsalted butter, melted
½ tsp. garlic bread seasoning mix

1. Pour 1 cup water into the pot. Push in the legs on the Crisper Tray, then place the tray in the bottom position in the pot. Spray a 8-inch round baking pan with cooking spray.
2. Cut the dinner rolls in slits and stuff cheese in the slits.
3. Top with butter and garlic bread seasoning mix.
4. Arrange the dinner rolls to the prepared pan, then place the pan on the tray.
5. Close the lid and flip the SmartSwitch to Rapid Cooker. Select STEAM & BAKE, set temperature to 350°F, and set time to 8 minutes. Press START/STOP to begin cooking (the unit will steam for approx. 4 minutes before baking).
6. When the time is up, dish out in a platter and serve hot.

Sunflower Seeds Bread

Prep: 15 minutes, Proof: 1 hour, Total Cook Time: 40 minutes, Steam: approx. 20 minutes, Cook: 20 minutes, Serves: 4

3 cups water, for steaming	cooking spray	1 cup lukewarm water
⅔ cup whole wheat flour	⅔ cup plain flour	½ sachet instant yeast
⅓ cup sunflower seeds	1 tsp. salt	

1. Pour 3 cups water into the pot. Push in the legs on the Crisper Tray, then place the tray in the bottom position in the pot. Spray a 8-inch round baking pan with cooking spray.

2. Mix together flours, sunflower seeds, yeast and salt in a bowl.

3. Add water slowly and knead for about 5 minutes until a dough is formed.

4. Place the dough on the baking pan and spray with cooking spray. Place the pan on the tray.

5. Close the lid and flip the SmartSwitch to Rapid Cooker. Select PROOF, set temperature to 95°F, and set time to 1 hour. Press START/STOP to begin proofing.

6. When proofing is complete, flip the SmartSwitch to Rapid Cooker. Select STEAM & BAKE, set temperature to 315°F, and set time to 20 minutes. Press START/STOP to begin cooking (the unit will steam for approx. 20 minutes before baking).

7. Dish out to serve warm.

Strawberry Cupcakes

Prep: 10 minutes, Total Cook Time: 18 minutes, Steam: approx. 10 minutes, Cook: 8 minutes, Serves: 8

1 cup water, for steaming	cooking spray	**FOR ICING:**
FOR CUPCAKES:		3½ tbsps. butter 1 cup icing sugar
7 tbsps. butter 2 eggs		¼ cup fresh strawberries, blended
7/8 cup self-rising flour ½ cup caster sugar		1 tbsp. whipped cream
½ tsp. vanilla essence		½ tsp. pink food color

1. Pour 1 cup water into the pot. Push in the legs on the Crisper Tray, then place the tray in the bottom position in the pot. Spray 8 muffin tins with cooking spray.

2. Mix all the ingredients for the cupcakes in a large bowl until well combined.

3. Transfer the mixture into muffin tins and place on the tray.

4. Close the lid and flip the SmartSwitch to Rapid Cooker. Select STEAM & BAKE, set temperature to 350°F, and set time to 8 minutes. Press START/STOP to begin cooking (the unit will steam for approx. 10 minutes before baking).

5. Mix all the ingredients for icing in a large bowl until well combined.

6. Fill the pastry bag with icing and top each cupcake evenly with frosting to serve.

Hummus Mushroom Pizza

Prep: 20 minutes, Total Cook Time: 28 minutes, Steam: approx. 20 minutes, Cook: 8 minutes, Serves: 4

1 cup water, for steaming   1 tsp. dried basil   4 Kalamata olives, sliced   ½ cup hummus

4 Portobello mushroom caps, stemmed and gills removed

1 tbsp. balsamic vinegar

Salt and black pepper, to taste

3 ounces zucchini, shredded   4 tbsps. pasta sauce   1 garlic clove, minced

2 tbsps. sweet red pepper, seeded and chopped

1. Pour 1 cup water into the pot. Push in the legs on the Crisper Tray, then place the tray in the bottom position in the pot. Spray a 8-inch round baking pan with cooking spray.

2. Coat both sides of all Portobello mushroom cap with vinegar.

3. Season the inside of each mushroom cap with salt and black pepper.

4. Divide pasta sauce and garlic inside each mushroom.

5. Arrange mushroom caps in the prepared pan, then place the pan on the tray.

6. Close the lid and flip the SmartSwitch to Rapid Cooker. Select STEAM & BAKE, set temperature to 330°F, and set time to 8 minutes. Press START/STOP to begin cooking (the unit will steam for approx. 20 minutes before baking).

7. With 4 minutes remaining, open the lid and top zucchini, red peppers and olives on each mushroom cap. Season with basil, salt, and black pepper. Close the lid to continue cooking.

8. Dish out in a serving platter. Spread hummus on each mushroom pizza and serve.

Pita Bread Cheese Pizza

Prep: 10 minutes, Total Cook Time: 21 minutes, Steam: approx. 15 minutes, Cook: 6 minutes, Serves: 4

1 cup water, for steaming   cooking spray   1 tbsp. pizza sauce

1 pita bread   ¼ cup Mozzarella cheese   1 drizzle extra-virgin olive oil

7 slices pepperoni   ¼ cup sausage   ½ tsp. fresh garlic, minced

1 tbsp. yellow onion, sliced thinly

1. Pour 1 cup water into the pot. Push in the legs on the Crisper Tray, then place the tray in the bottom position in the pot. Spray a 8-inch round baking pan with cooking spray.

2. Spread pizza sauce on the pita bread and add sausages, pepperoni, onions, garlic and cheese.

3. Drizzle with olive oil and transfer the pita bread to the prepared pan, then place the pan on the tray.

4. Close the lid and flip the SmartSwitch to Rapid Cooker. Select STEAM & BAKE, set temperature to 350°F, and set time to 6 minutes. Press START/STOP to begin cooking (the unit will steam for approx. 15 minutes before baking).

5. Dish out to serve warm.

Simple Donuts

Prep: 10 minutes, Total Cook Time: 30 minutes, Steam: approx. 20 minutes, Cook: 10 minutes, Serves: 3

1 cup water, for steaming	cooking spray	1 tbsp. butter, softened	½ cup milk
2 cups all-purpose flour	1 egg	Salt, to taste	¾ cup sugar
2 tsps. baking powder		2 tsps. vanilla extract	2 tbsps. icing sugar

1. Pour 1 cup water into the pot. Push in the legs on the Crisper Tray, then place the tray in the bottom position in the pot. Spray a 8-inch round baking pan with cooking spray.

2. Sift together flour, baking powder and salt in a large bowl.

3. Add sugar and egg and mix well.

4. Stir in the butter, milk and vanilla extract and mix until a dough is formed.

5. Refrigerate the dough for at least 1 hour and roll the dough into ½ inch thickness onto a floured surface.

6. Cut into donuts with a donut cutter and arrange the donuts on the baking pan(You may need cook in two batches). Place the pan on the tray.

7. Close the lid and flip the SmartSwitch to Rapid Cooker. Select STEAM & BAKE, set temperature to 375°F, and set time to 10 minutes. Press START/STOP to begin cooking (the unit will steam for approx. 20 minutes before baking), until golden.

8. Serve warm.

Cheese Stuffed Tomatoes

Prep: 15 minutes, Total Cook Time: 30 minutes, Steam: approx. 15 minutes, Cook: 15 minutes, Serves: 2

1 cup water, for steaming	cooking spray	½ cup cheddar cheese, shredded
2 large tomatoes, sliced in half and pulp scooped out		1 tbsp. unsalted butter, melted
½ cup broccoli, finely chopped		½ tsp. dried thyme, crushed

1. Pour 1 cup water into the pot. Push in the legs on the Crisper Tray, then place the tray in the bottom position in the pot. Spray a 8-inch round baking pan with cooking spray.

2. Mix together broccoli and cheese in a bowl.

3. Stuff the broccoli mixture in each tomato.

4. Arrange the stuffed tomatoes to the prepared pan and drizzle evenly with butter. Then place the pan on the tray.

5. Close the lid and flip the SmartSwitch to Rapid Cooker. Select STEAM & BAKE, set temperature to 350°F, and set time to 15 minutes. Press START/STOP to begin cooking (the unit will steam for approx. 15 minutes before baking).

6. Dish out in a serving platter.

7. Garnish with thyme and serve warm.

AIR FRY

Dill Pickle Fries

Prep Time: 15 minutes, Cook Time: 24 minutes, Serves: 12

cooking spray 1 cup all-purpose flour   1 egg, beaten   ½ tsp. paprika

1½ (16-ounces) jars spicy dill pickle spears, drained   ¼ cup milk   1 cup panko breadcrumbs
and pat dried

1. Push in the legs on the Crisper Tray, then place the tray in the bottom of the pot. Spray the tray with cooking spray.
2. Place flour and paprika in a shallow dish and whisk the egg with milk in a second dish.
3. Place the breadcrumbs in a third shallow dish.
4. Coat the pickle spears evenly in flour and dip in the egg mixture. Roll into the breadcrumbs evenly.
5. Close the lid and flip the SmartSwitch to AIRFRY/STOVETOP. Select AIRFRY, set temperature to 390°F, and set time to 17 minutes (unit will need to preheat for 5 minutes, so set an external timer if desired). Press START/STOP to begin cooking.
6. When the unit is preheated and the time reaches 12 minutes, place the half of the pickle spears on the tray. Close the lid to begin cooking.
7. After 5 minutes, open the lid and flip the pickle spears once with silicone-tipped tongs to ensure even cooking. Close the lid to continue cooking.
8. Repeat with the remaining pickle spears and dish out to serve warm.

Air Fried Plantains

Prep Time: 10 minutes, Cook Time: 8 minutes, Serves: 4

cooking spray 2 ripe plantains   2 tsps. avocado oil   ⅛ tsp. salt

1. Push in the legs on the Crisper Tray, then place the tray in the bottom of the pot. Spray the tray with cooking spray.
2. Mix the plantains with avocado oil and salt in a bowl.
3. Close the lid and flip the SmartSwitch to AIRFRY/STOVETOP. Select AIRFRY, set temperature to 390°F, and set time to 13 minutes (unit will need to preheat for 5 minutes, so set an external timer if desired). Press START/STOP to begin cooking.
4. When the unit is preheated and the time reaches 8 minutes, place the coated plantains on the tray. Close the lid to begin cooking.
5. After 4 minutes, open the lid and toss the plantains with silicone-tipped tongs to ensure even cooking. Close the lid to continue cooking.
6. When cooking is complete, serve immediately.

Old-Fashioned Eggplant Slices

Prep Time: 10 minutes, Cook Time: 8 minutes, Serves: 2

cooking spray   ½ cup all-purpose flour

1 medium eggplant, peeled and cut into ½-inch round slices

1 cup Italian-style breadcrumbs

2 eggs, beaten   2 tbsps. milk

Salt, to taste   ¼ cup olive oil

1. Push in the legs on the Crisper Tray, then place the tray in the bottom of the pot. Spray the tray with cooking spray.

2. Season the eggplant slices with salt and keep aside for 1 hour.

3. Place flour in a shallow dish.

4. Whisk the eggs with milk in a second dish.

5. Mix together oil and breadcrumbs in a third shallow dish.

6. Coat the eggplant slices evenly with flour, then dip in the egg mixture and finally coat with breadcrumb mixture.

7. Close the lid and flip the SmartSwitch to AIRFRY/STOVETOP. Select AIRFRY, set temperature to 390°F, and set time to 13 minutes (unit will need to preheat for 5 minutes, so set an external timer if desired). Press START/STOP to begin cooking.

8. When the unit is preheated and the time reaches 8 minutes, place the eggplant slices on the tray. Close the lid to begin cooking.

9. When cooking is complete, serve hot.

Old-Fashioned Onion Rings

Prep Time: 10 minutes, Cook Time: 10 minutes, Serves: 4

cooking spray   1 large onion, cut into rings

1¼ cups all-purpose flour   1 cup milk

1 egg   ¾ cup dry bread crumbs

Salt, to taste

1. Push in the legs on the Crisper Tray, then place the tray in the bottom of the pot. Spray the tray with cooking spray.

2. Mix together flour and salt in a dish.

3. Whisk egg with milk in a second dish until well mixed.

4. Place the breadcrumbs in a third dish.

5. Coat the onion rings with the flour mixture and dip into the egg mixture. Lastly dredge in the breadcrumbs.

6. Close the lid and flip the SmartSwitch to AIRFRY/STOVETOP. Select AIRFRY, set temperature to 390°F, and set time to 15 minutes (unit will need to preheat for 5 minutes, so set an external timer if desired). Press START/STOP to begin cooking.

7. When the unit is preheated and the time reaches 10 minutes, place the onion rings on the tray. Close the lid to begin cooking.

8. After 5 minutes, open the lid and flip the onion rings with silicone-tipped tongs to ensure even cooking. Close the lid to continue cooking.

9. When cooking is complete, serve hot.

Air Fried Chicken Tenders

Prep Time: 15 minutes, Cook Time: 18 minutes, Serves: 4

cooking spray
12 oz chicken breasts, cut into tenders

1 egg white
⅛ cup flour

Salt and black pepper, to taste
½ cup panko bread crumbs

1. Push in the legs on the Crisper Tray, then place the tray in the bottom of the pot. Spray the tray with cooking spray.
2. Season the chicken tenders with salt and black pepper.
3. Coat the chicken tenders with flour, then dip in egg whites and then dredge in the panko bread crumbs.
4. Close the lid and flip the SmartSwitch to AIRFRY/STOVETOP. Select AIRFRY, set temperature to 375°F, and set time to 23 minutes (unit will need to preheat for 5 minutes, so set an external timer if desired). Press START/STOP to begin cooking.
5. When the unit is preheated and the time reaches 18 minutes, place the chicken tenders on the tray. Close the lid to begin cooking.
6. After 10 minutes, open the lid and toss the chicken tenders with silicone-tipped tongs to ensure even cooking. Close the lid to continue cooking.
7. When the time is up, serve chicken tenders hot.

Beet Chips

Prep Time: 10 minutes, Cook Time: 15 minutes, Serves: 6

cooking spray   2 tbsps. olive oil
4 medium beets, peeled and thinly sliced

¼ tsp. smoked paprika   ½ tsp. salt

1. Push in the legs on the Crisper Tray, then place the tray in the bottom of the pot. Spray the tray with cooking spray.
2. Mix together all the ingredients in a bowl until well combined.
3. Close the lid and flip the SmartSwitch to AIRFRY/STOVETOP. Select AIRFRY, set temperature to 390°F, and set time to 20 minutes (unit will need to preheat for 5 minutes, so set an external timer if desired). Press START/STOP to begin cooking.
4. When the unit is preheated and the time reaches 15 minutes, place the beet slices on the tray. Close the lid to begin cooking.
5. After 8 minutes, open the lid and toss the beet slices with silicone-tipped tongs to ensure even cooking. Close the lid to continue cooking.
6. When cooking is complete, serve warm.

Crunchy Spicy Chickpeas

Prep Time: 5 minutes, Cook Time: 15 minutes, Serves: 4

cooking spray   ½ tsp. smoked paprika
1 (15-ounce) can chickpeas, rinsed and drained

1 tbsp. olive oil   ½ tsp. ground cumin
½ tsp. cayenne pepper   Salt, taste

1. Push in the legs on the Crisper Tray, then place the tray in the bottom of the pot. Spray the tray with cooking spray.
2. Mix together all the ingredients in a bowl and toss to coat well.
3. Close the lid and flip the SmartSwitch to AIRFRY/STOVETOP. Select AIRFRY, set temperature to 390°F, and set time to 20 minutes (unit will need to preheat for 5 minutes, so set an external timer if desired). Press START/STOP to begin cooking.
4. When the unit is preheated and the time reaches 15 minutes, place the chickpeas on the tray. Close the lid to begin cooking.
5. After 8 minutes, open the lid and toss the chickpeas with silicone-tipped tongs to ensure even cooking. Close the lid to continue cooking.
6. When cooking is complete, serve warm.

Air Fried Zucchini Gratin

Prep Time: 10 minutes, Cook Time: 17 minutes, Serves: 4

cooking spray   2 tbsps. bread crumbs
2 zucchinis, cut into 8 equal sized pieces
1 tbsp. fresh parsley, chopped
4 tbsps. Parmesan cheese, grated

1 tbsp. vegetable oil
Salt and black pepper, to taste

1. Push in the legs on the Crisper Tray, then place the tray in the bottom of the pot. Spray the tray with cooking spray.
2. Close the lid and flip the SmartSwitch to AIRFRY/STOVETOP. Select AIRFRY, set temperature to 390°F, and set time to 22 minutes (unit will need to preheat for 5 minutes, so set an external timer if desired). Press START/STOP to begin cooking.
3. When the unit is preheated and the time reaches 17 minutes, place the zucchini pieces on the tray with their skin side down. Close the lid to begin cooking.
4. After 10 minutes, open the lid and toss the zucchini pieces with silicone-tipped tongs to ensure even cooking. Close the lid to continue cooking.
5. When cooking is complete, serve warm.

Butternut Squash Fries

Prep Time: 15 minutes, Cook Time: 40 minutes, Serves: 2

cooking spray   1 tsp. chili powder   ½ tsp. ground cinnamon   ¼ tsp. garlic salt

1. 2 pounds butternut squash, peeled and cut into ½ inch strips
2. Push in the legs on the Crisper Tray, then place the tray in the bottom of the pot. Spray the tray with cooking spray.
3. Season butternut squash with all other ingredients in a bowl until well combined.
4. Close the lid and flip the SmartSwitch to AIRFRY/STOVETOP. Select AIRFRY, set temperature to 390°F, and set time to 25 minutes (unit will need to preheat for 5 minutes, so set an external timer if desired). Press START/STOP to begin cooking.
5. When the unit is preheated and the time reaches 20 minutes, place half of the squash fries on the tray. Close the lid to begin cooking.
6. After 10 minutes, open the lid and toss the squash fries with silicone-tipped tongs to ensure even cooking. Close the lid to continue cooking.
7. Repeat with the remaining fries and dish out to serve warm.

Easy Crispy Prawns

Prep Time: 15 minutes, Cook Time: 10 minutes, Serves: 4

cooking spray   1 egg
½ pound nacho chips, crushed

18 prawns, peeled and deveined
Salt and black pepper, to taste

1. Push in the legs on the Crisper Tray, then place the tray in the bottom of the pot. Spray the tray with cooking spray.
2. Crack egg in a shallow dish and beat well.
3. Place the crushed nacho chips in another shallow dish.
4. Coat prawns with egg, salt and black pepper, then roll into nacho chips.
5. Close the lid and flip the SmartSwitch to AIRFRY/STOVETOP. Select AIRFRY, set temperature to 390°F, and set time to 15 minutes (unit will need to preheat for 5 minutes, so set an external timer if desired). Press START/STOP to begin cooking.
6. When the unit is preheated and the time reaches 10 minutes, place the coated prawns on the tray. Close the lid to begin cooking.
7. After 5 minutes, open the lid and toss the coated prawns with silicone-tipped tongs to ensure even cooking. Close the lid to continue cooking.
8. When cooking is complete, serve hot.

Simple Banana Chips

Prep Time: 10 minutes, Cook Time: 10 minutes, Serves: 8

cooking spray   2 tbsps. olive oil   Salt and black pepper, to taste
2 raw bananas, peeled and sliced

1. Push in the legs on the Crisper Tray, then place the tray in the bottom of the pot. Spray the tray with cooking spray.
2. Drizzle banana slices evenly with olive oil.
3. Close the lid and flip the SmartSwitch to AIRFRY/STOVETOP. Select AIRFRY, set temperature to 390°F, and set time to 15 minutes (unit will need to preheat for 5 minutes, so set an external timer if desired). Press START/STOP to begin cooking.
4. When the unit is preheated and the time reaches 10 minutes, place the banana slices on the tray. Close the lid to begin cooking.
5. After 5 minutes, open the lid and season with salt and black pepper. Toss the banana slices with silicone-tipped tongs to ensure even cooking. Close the lid to continue cooking.
6. When cooking is complete, serve hot.

Apple Dumplings

Prep Time: 10 minutes, Cook Time: 15 minutes, Serves: 2

cooking spray   2 sheets puff pastry   2 tbsps. raisins 2 tbsps. butter, melted
2 small apples, peeled and cored   1 tbsp. brown sugar

1. Push in the legs on the Crisper Tray, then place the tray in the bottom of the pot. Spray the tray with cooking spray.
2. Mix sugar and raisins in a bowl and fill each apple core with it.
3. Place the apple in the center of each pastry sheet and fold to completely cover the apple. Seal the edges.
4. Close the lid and flip the SmartSwitch to AIRFRY/STOVETOP. Select AIRFRY, set temperature to 390°F, and set time to 20 minutes (unit will need to preheat for 5 minutes, so set an external timer if desired). Press START/STOP to begin cooking.
5. When the unit is preheated and the time reaches 15 minutes, place the dumplings on the tray. Close the lid to begin cooking.
6. After 8 minutes, open the lid and toss the dumplings with silicone-tipped tongs to ensure even cooking. Close the lid to continue cooking.
7. When cooking is complete, serve hot.

Crispy Kale Chips

Prep Time: 10 minutes, Cook Time: 8 minutes, Serves: 4

cooking spray   1 tbsp. olive oil   1 tsp. soy sauce
1 head fresh kale, stems and ribs removed and cut into 1½ inch pieces

1. Push in the legs on the Crisper Tray, then place the tray in the bottom of the pot. Spray the tray with cooking spray.
2. Mix together all the ingredients in a bowl until well combined.
3. Close the lid and flip the SmartSwitch to AIRFRY/STOVETOP. Select AIRFRY, set temperature to 300°F, and set time to 13 minutes (unit will need to preheat for 5 minutes, so set an external timer if desired). Press START/STOP to begin cooking.
4. When the unit is preheated and the time reaches 8 minutes, place the kale on the tray. Close the lid to begin cooking.
5. After 4 minutes, open the lid and flip the kale with silicone-tipped tongs to ensure even cooking. Close the lid to continue cooking.
6. When cooking is complete, serve warm.

Crispy Shrimps

Prep Time: 15 minutes, Cook Time: 7 minutes, Serves: 2

cooking spray	1 egg	10 shrimps, peeled and deveined
¼ pound nacho chips, crushed		Salt and black pepper, to taste

1. Push in the legs on the Crisper Tray, then place the tray in the bottom of the pot. Spray the tray with cooking spray.

2. Crack egg in a shallow dish and beat well.

3. Place the nacho chips in another shallow dish.

4. Season the shrimps with salt and black pepper, coat into egg and then roll into nacho chips.

5. Close the lid and flip the SmartSwitch to AIRFRY/STOVETOP. Select AIRFRY, set temperature to 390°F, and set time to 12 minutes (unit will need to preheat for 5 minutes, so set an external timer if desired). Press START/STOP to begin cooking.

6. When the unit is preheated and the time reaches 7 minutes, place the shrimps on the tray. Close the lid to begin cooking.

7. After 4 minutes, open the lid and flip the shrimps with silicone-tipped tongs to ensure even cooking. Close the lid to continue cooking.

8. When cooking is complete, serve warm.

Avocado Fries

Prep Time: 20 minutes, Cook Time: 9 minutes, Serves: 2

cooking spray	¼ cup all-purpose flour	1 avocado, peeled, pitted and sliced into 8 pieces
1 egg	1 tsp. water	Salt and black pepper, to taste
½ cup panko breadcrumbs		

1. Push in the legs on the Crisper Tray, then place the tray in the bottom of the pot. Spray the tray with cooking spray.

2. Place flour, salt and black pepper in a shallow dish and whisk the egg with water in a second dish.

3. Place the breadcrumbs in a third shallow dish.

4. Coat the avocado slices evenly in flour and dip in the egg mixture. Roll into the breadcrumbs evenly.

5. Close the lid and flip the SmartSwitch to AIRFRY/STOVETOP. Select AIRFRY, set temperature to 400°F, and set time to 14 minutes (unit will need to preheat for 5 minutes, so set an external timer if desired). Press START/STOP to begin cooking.

6. When the unit is preheated and the time reaches 9 minutes, place the avocado slices on the tray. Close the lid to begin cooking.

7. After 5 minutes, open the lid and toss the avocado slices with silicone-tipped tongs to ensure even cooking. Close the lid to continue cooking.

8. When cooking is complete, serve hot.

BAKE&ROAST

Basic Butter Cookies

Prep Time: 10 minutes, Cook Time: 10 minutes, Serves: 8

cooking spray   4-ounce unsalted butter   1¼-ounce icing sugar
1 cup all-purpose flour   ¼ tsp. baking powder

1. Push in the legs on the Crisper Tray, then place the tray in the bottom of the pot. Spray a 8-inch round baking pan with cooking spray.
2. Mix butter, icing sugar, flour and baking powder in a large bowl.
3. Mix well until a dough is formed and transfer into the piping bag fitted with a fluted nozzle. Pipe the dough onto the baking pan.
4. Close the lid and flip the SmartSwitch to AIRFRY/STOVETOP. Select BAKE & ROAST, set temperature to 340°F, and set time to 15 minutes (unit will need to preheat for 5 minutes, so set an external timer if desired). Press START/STOP to begin cooking.
5. When the unit is preheated and the time reaches 10 minutes, place the pan on the tray. Close the lid to begin cooking, until golden brown.
6. Let cool for about 5 minutes on a wire rack.
7. Serve with tea.

Classic Buttermilk Biscuits

Prep Time: 15 minutes, Cook Time: 8 minutes, Serves: 4

cooking spray   ½ cup cake flour   ¼ cup + 2 tbsps. butter, cut into cubes
1¼ cups all-purpose flour   ¾ cup buttermilk   1 tsp. granulated sugar
¾ tsp. baking powder   Salt, to taste

1. Push in the legs on the Crisper Tray, then place the tray in the bottom of the pot. Spray a 8-inch round baking pan with cooking spray.
2. Sift together flours, baking soda, baking powder, sugar and salt in a large bowl.
3. Add cold butter and mix until a coarse crumb is formed.
4. Stir in the buttermilk slowly and mix until a dough is formed.
5. Press the dough into ½ inch thickness onto a floured surface and cut out circles with a 1¾-inch round cookie cutter.
6. Arrange the biscuits in the baking pan in a single layer and brush butter on them.
7. Close the lid and flip the SmartSwitch to AIRFRY/STOVETOP. Select BAKE & ROAST, set temperature to 400°F, and set time to 13 minutes (unit will need to preheat for 5 minutes, so set an external timer if desired). Press START/STOP to begin cooking.
8. When the unit is preheated and the time reaches 8 minutes, place the pan on the tray. Close the lid to begin cooking.
9. Serve warm.

Healthy Fruit Muffins

Prep Time: 10 minutes, Cook Time: 10 minutes, Serves: 6

1 cup milk ¾ tsp. baking powder	1 tsp. cocoa powder 1 tsp. honey
1 pack Oreo biscuits, crushed	1 tsp. fresh lemon juice
1 banana, peeled and chopped	Pinch of ground cinnamon
1 apple, peeled, cored and chopped	

1. Push in the legs on the Crisper Tray, then place the tray in the bottom of the pot. Spray 6 muffin cups with cooking spray.

2. Mix milk, biscuits, cocoa powder, baking soda and baking powder in a bowl until a smooth mixture is formed.

3. Divide this mixture into the prepared muffin cups.

4. Close the lid and flip the SmartSwitch to AIRFRY/STOVETOP. Select BAKE & ROAST, set temperature to 350°F, and set time to 15 minutes (unit will need to preheat for 5 minutes, so set an external timer if desired). Press START/STOP to begin cooking.

5. When the unit is preheated and the time reaches 10 minutes, place the muffin cups on the tray. Close the lid to begin cooking.

6. Mix banana, apple, honey, lemon juice and cinnamon in a bowl.

7. Scoop out some portion from center of muffins and fill with the fruit mixture.

8. Refrigerate for 2 hours and serve chilled.

Flank Steak Beef

Prep Time: 10 minutes, Cook Time: 12 minutes, Serves: 4

cooking spray ¼ cup xanthum gum	½ cup soy sauce 1 tbsp. garlic, minced
1 pound flank steaks, sliced	½ cup water ¾ cup swerve, packed
2 tsp. vegetable oil ½ tsp. ginger	

1. Push in the legs on the Crisper Tray, then place the tray in the bottom of the pot. Spray the tray with cooking spray.

2. Coat the steaks with xanthum gum on both the sides.

3. Close the lid and flip the SmartSwitch to AIRFRY/STOVETOP. Select BAKE & ROAST, set temperature to 390°F, and set time to 17 minutes (unit will need to preheat for 5 minutes, so set an external timer if desired). Press START/STOP to begin cooking.

4. When the unit is preheated and the time reaches 12 minutes, place the steaks on the tray. Close the lid to begin cooking.

5. After 6 minutes, open the lid and flip the steaks with silicone-tipped tongs to ensure even cooking. Close the lid to continue cooking.

6. Meanwhile, cook rest of the ingredients for the sauce in a saucepan.

7. Bring to a boil and pour over the steak slices to serve.

Garlicky Lamb Chops

Prep Time: 20 minutes, Cook Time: 32 minutes, Serves: 4

cooking spray   ¼ cup olive oil, divided

1 tbsp. fresh oregano, chopped

1 tbsp. fresh thyme, chopped

8 (4-ounce) lamb chops

1 bulb garlic   Salt and black pepper, to taste

1. Push in the legs on the Crisper Tray, then place the tray in the bottom of the pot. Spray the tray with cooking spray.

2. Rub the garlic bulb with about 2 tbsps. of the olive oil.

3. Close the lid and flip the SmartSwitch to AIRFRY/STOVETOP. Select BAKE & ROAST, set temperature to 390°F, and set time to 17 minutes (unit will need to preheat for 5 minutes, so set an external timer if desired). Press START/STOP to begin cooking.

4. When the unit is preheated and the time reaches 12 minutes, place the garlic bulb on the tray. Close the lid to begin cooking.

5. Mix remaining oil, herbs, salt and black pepper in a large bowl.

6. Coat the lamb chops with about 1 tbsp. of the herb mixture.

7. When cooking is complete, place half of the chops on the tray with garlic bulb and roast for 10 minutes.

8. Repeat with the remaining lamb chops and serve with herb mixture.

Cheesy Beef Meatballs

Prep Time: 20 minutes, Cook Time: 24 minutes, Serves: 8

2 pounds ground beef   1¼ cups breadcrumbs

¼ cup Parmigiana-Reggiano cheese, grated

2 large eggs   ¼ cup fresh parsley, chopped

1 small garlic clove, chopped

1 tsp. dried oregano, crushed

Salt and black pepper, to taste

1. Push in the legs on the Crisper Tray, then place the tray in the bottom of the pot. Spray the tray with cooking spray.

2. Mix all the ingredients in a bowl until well combined.

3. Shape the mixture into 2-inches balls.

4. Close the lid and flip the SmartSwitch to AIRFRY/STOVETOP. Select BAKE & ROAST, set temperature to 390°F, and set time to 17 minutes (unit will need to preheat for 5 minutes, so set an external timer if desired). Press START/STOP to begin cooking.

5. When the unit is preheated and the time reaches 12 minutes, place half of the meatballs on the tray. Close the lid to begin cooking.

6. After 6 minutes, open the lid and flip the side with silicone-tipped tongs to ensure even cooking. Close the lid to continue cooking.

7. Repeat with the remaining meatballs and serve warm.

Herbed Lamb Chops

Prep Time: 10 minutes, Cook Time: 15 minutes, Serves: 2

cooking spray   4 (4-ounces) lamb chops   1 tsp. dried oregano   ½ tsp. ground cumin

1 tbsp. fresh lemon juice   1 tbsp. olive oil   ½ tsp. ground coriander

1 tsp. dried rosemary   1 tsp. dried thyme   Salt and black pepper, to taste

1. Push in the legs on the Crisper Tray, then place the tray in the bottom of the pot. Spray the tray with cooking spray.

2. Mix the lemon juice, oil, herbs, and spices in a large bowl.

3. Coat the chops generously with the herb mixture and refrigerate to marinate for about 1 hour.

4. Close the lid and flip the SmartSwitch to AIRFRY/STOVETOP. Select BAKE & ROAST, set temperature to 390°F, and set time to 20 minutes (unit will need to preheat for 5 minutes, so set an external timer if desired). Press START/STOP to begin cooking.

5. When the unit is preheated and the time reaches 15 minutes, place the chops on the tray. Close the lid to begin cooking.

6. After 5 minutes, open the lid and flip the chops with silicone-tipped tongs to ensure even cooking. Close the lid to continue cooking.

7. When cooking is complete, serve hot.

Vanilla Soufflé

Prep Time: 15 minutes, Cook Time: 40 minutes, Serves: 6

cooking spray   ¼ cup butter, softened   ½ cup sugar   3 tsps. vanilla extract, divided

¼ cup all-purpose flour   1 cup milk   1 tsp. cream of tartar   1-ounce sugar

4 egg yolks   5 egg whites

1. Push in the legs on the Crisper Tray, then place the tray in the bottom of the pot. Spray 6 ramekins with cooking spray.

2. Mix butter and flour in a bowl until a smooth paste is formed.

3. Put milk and ½ cup of sugar in a bowl and cook for about 3 minutes on medium-low heat in a pan.

4. Bring to a boil and stir in the flour mixture.

5. Let it simmer for about 4 minutes and remove from heat.

6. Whisk egg yolks and vanilla extract in a bowl until well combined.

7. Combine the egg yolk mixture with milk mixture until mixed.

8. Mix egg whites, cream of tartar, remaining sugar and vanilla extract in another bowl.

9. Combine the egg white mixture into milk mixture and divide this mixture into the ramekins.

10. Close the lid and flip the SmartSwitch to AIRFRY/STOVETOP. Select BAKE & ROAST, set temperature to 330°F, and set time to 21 minutes (unit will need to preheat for 5 minutes, so set an external timer if desired). Press START/STOP to begin cooking.

11. When the unit is preheated and the time reaches 16 minutes, place 3 ramekins on the tray. Close the lid to begin cooking.

12. Repeat with the remaining ramekins and dish out to serve.

Party Time Mixed Nuts

Prep Time: 15 minutes, Cook Time: 14 minutes, Serves: 3

cooking spray   ½ cup raw peanuts   ½ cup raisins   ½ cup pecans

½ cup raw almonds   1 tbsp. olive oil Salt, to taste

½ cup raw cashew nuts

1. Push in the legs on the Crisper Tray, then place the tray in the bottom of the pot. Spray the tray with cooking spray.
2. Close the lid and flip the SmartSwitch to AIRFRY/STOVETOP. Select BAKE & ROAST, set temperature to 320°F, and set time to 14 minutes (unit will need to preheat for 5 minutes, so set an external timer if desired). Press START/STOP to begin cooking.
3. When the unit is preheated and the time reaches 9 minutes, place the nuts on the tray. Close the lid to begin cooking.
4. When cooking is complete, drizzle with olive oil and salt and toss to coat well.
5. Return the nuts mixture on the tray and roast for 5 minutes.
6. Serve warm.

Super Simple Steaks

Prep Time: 5 minutes, Cook Time: 14 minutes, Serves: 2

cooking spray   ½ pound quality cuts steak   Salt and black pepper, to taste

1. Push in the legs on the Crisper Tray, then place the tray in the bottom of the pot. Spray the tray with cooking spray.
2. Season the steaks evenly with salt and black pepper.
3. Close the lid and flip the SmartSwitch to AIRFRY/STOVETOP. Select BAKE & ROAST, set temperature to 390°F, and set time to 19 minutes (unit will need to preheat for 5 minutes, so set an external timer if desired). Press START/STOP to begin cooking.
4. When the unit is preheated and the time reaches 14 minutes, place the steaks on the tray. Close the lid to begin cooking.
5. After 7 minutes, open the lid and flip the steaks with silicone-tipped tongs to ensure even cooking. Close the lid to continue cooking.
6. When cooking is complete, serve hot.

Grilled Cheese Sandwiches

Prep Time: 10 minutes, Cook Time: 7 minutes, Serves: 2

cooking spray   4 white bread slices   ½ cup sharp cheddar cheese, grated

½ cup melted butter, softened   1 tbsp. mayonnaise

1. Push in the legs on the Crisper Tray, then place the tray in the bottom of the pot. Spray the tray with cooking spray.
2. Spread the mayonnaise and melted butter over one side of each bread slice.
3. Sprinkle the cheddar cheese over the buttered side of the 2 slices. Cover with the remaining slices of bread.
4. Close the lid and flip the SmartSwitch to AIRFRY/STOVETOP. Select BAKE & ROAST, set temperature to 355°F, and set time to 12 minutes (unit will need to preheat for 5 minutes, so set an external timer if desired). Press START/STOP to begin cooking.
5. When the unit is preheated and the time reaches 7 minutes, place the sandwiches on the tray. Close the lid to begin cooking.
6. When cooking is complete, serve hot.

Beef Chuck with Brussels Sprouts

Prep Time: 20 minutes, Cook Time: 25 minutes, Serves: 4

1 pound (454 g) beef chuck shoulder steak

2 tbsps. vegetable oil   1 tbsp. red wine vinegar

1 tsp. fine sea salt   ½ tsp. ground black pepper

1 tsp. smoked paprika   1 tsp. onion powder

½ tsp. garlic powder   ½ tsp. fennel seeds

½ pound (227 g) Brussels sprouts, cleaned and halved

1 tsp. dried basil   1 tsp. dried sage

1. Push in the legs on the Crisper Tray, then place the tray in the bottom of the pot. Spray the tray with cooking spray.

2. Massage the beef with the vegetable oil, wine vinegar, salt, black pepper, paprika, onion powder, and garlic powder, coating it well.

3. Allow to marinate for a minimum of 3 hours.

4. Close the lid and flip the SmartSwitch to AIRFRY/STOVETOP. Select BAKE & ROAST, set temperature to 390°F, and set time to 15 minutes (unit will need to preheat for 5 minutes, so set an external timer if desired). Press START/STOP to begin cooking.

5. When the unit is preheated and the time reaches 10 minutes, remove the beef from the marinade and put on the tray. Close the lid to begin cooking.

6. After 5 minutes, open the lid and flip the beef with silicone-tipped tongs to ensure even cooking. Close the lid to continue cooking.

7. When cooking is complete, put the prepared Brussels sprouts on the tray along with the fennel seeds, basil, and sage.

8. Roast everything for another 5 minutes.

9. Give them a good stir. Roast for an additional 10 minutes.

Beef Loin with Thyme and Parsley

Prep Time: 5 minutes, Cook Time: 15 minutes, Serves: 4

cooking spray   1 tbsp. butter, melted

¼ dried thyme   1 tsp. garlic salt

¼ tsp. dried parsley   1 pound (454 g) beef loin

1. Push in the legs on the Crisper Tray, then place the tray in the bottom of the pot. Spray the tray with cooking spray.

2. In a bowl, combine the melted butter, thyme, garlic salt, and parsley.

3. Cut the beef loin into slices and generously apply the seasoned butter using a brush.

4. Close the lid and flip the SmartSwitch to AIRFRY/STOVETOP. Select BAKE & ROAST, set temperature to 400°F, and set time to 20 minutes (unit will need to preheat for 5 minutes, so set an external timer if desired). Press START/STOP to begin cooking.

5. When the unit is preheated and the time reaches 15 minutes, place the beef on the tray. Close the lid to begin cooking.

6. After 8 minutes, open the lid and flip the beef with silicone-tipped tongs to ensure even cooking. Close the lid to continue cooking.

7. Take care when removing it and serve hot.

Cheddar Bacon Burst with Spinach

Prep Time: 5 minutes, Cook Time: 30 minutes, Serves: 8

30 slices bacon   1 tbsp. Chipotle seasoning   2½ cups Cheddar cheese

2 tsps. Italian seasoning   4 cups raw spinach

1. Push in the legs on the Crisper Tray, then place the tray in the bottom of the pot.

2. Weave the bacon into 15 vertical pieces and 12 horizontal pieces. Cut the extra 3 in half to fill in the rest, horizontally.

3. Season the bacon with Chipotle seasoning and Italian seasoning.

4. Add the cheese to the bacon.

5. Add the spinach and press down to compress.

6. Tightly roll up the woven bacon.

7. Line a baking sheet with kitchen foil and add plenty of salt to it.

8. Put the bacon on top of a cooling rack.

9. Close the lid and flip the SmartSwitch to AIRFRY/STOVETOP. Select BAKE & ROAST, set temperature to 350°F, and set time to 35 minutes (unit will need to preheat for 5 minutes, so set an external timer if desired). Press START/STOP to begin cooking.

10. When the unit is preheated and the time reaches 30 minutes, place the rack with bacon on the tray. Close the lid to begin cooking.

11. Let cool for 15 minutes before slicing and serve.

Marinated Pork Tenderloin

Prep Time: 10 minutes, Cook Time: 30 minutes, Serves: 4 to 6

cooking spray   ¼ cup olive oil   1 tbsp. Dijon mustard   1 tsp. salt

¼ cup soy sauce   1 garlic clove, minced   ½ tsp. freshly ground black pepper

¼ cup freshly squeezed lemon juice   2 pounds (907 g) pork tenderloin

1. Push in the legs on the Crisper Tray, then place the tray in the bottom of the pot. Spray the tray with cooking spray.

2. In a large mixing bowl, make the marinade: Mix the olive oil, soy sauce, lemon juice, minced garlic, Dijon mustard, salt, and pepper. Reserve ¼ cup of the marinade.

3. Put the tenderloin in a large bowl and pour the remaining marinade over the meat. Cover and marinate in the refrigerator for about 1 hour.

4. Close the lid and flip the SmartSwitch to AIRFRY/STOVETOP. Select BAKE & ROAST, set temperature to 375°F, and set time to 35 minutes (unit will need to preheat for 5 minutes, so set an external timer if desired). Press START/STOP to begin cooking.

5. When the unit is preheated and the time reaches 30 minutes, place the marinated pork tenderloin on the tray. Close the lid to begin cooking.

6. With 20 minutes remaining, open the lid. Flip the pork and baste it with half of the reserved marinade. Close the lid to continue cooking. Repeat this process when 10 minutes remain.

7. When cooking is complete, serve hot.

DEHYDRATE

Bananas

Prep Time: 10 minutes, Cook Time: 7 hours, Serves: 4

spray bottle of lemon juice
4 medium bananas, peeled and cut across into ⅛-inch-thick slices

1. Lightly spray the banana slices with lemon juice, spread on dehydrator rack.
2. Push in the legs on the Crisper Tray, then place the tray in the bottom position in the pot. Put the rack with banana chips on the tray.
3. Close the lid and flip the SmartSwitch to AIRFRY/STOVETOP. Select DEHYDRATE, set temperature to 135°F, and set time to 7 hours. Press START/STOP to begin cooking. When done, the banana chips should be brittle, feel dry to the touch, and snap in half easily.
4. Remove the banana chips from the cooker, serve immediately ou vacuum seal in vacuum bags with an oxygen pack, and then double-bagged in Mylar bag.

Sweet and Spicy Pepper Beef Jerky

Prep Time: 20 minutes, Cook Time: 6 hours 15 minutes, Makes: ½ pound jerky

1½ pounds beef eye of round
½ cup pineapple juice
¼ cup firmly packed brown sugar
¼ cup soy sauce
1 tbsp. crushed dehydrated jalapeños
1 tsp. hot sauce

1. Trim the meat of any visible fat, then partially freeze. Cut into ¼-inch-thick slices or strips across the grain using a very sharp knife or meat slicer. Try to cut the meat as uniformly as possible for even drying. Place the strips in a large ziptop plastic freezer bag.
2. While the meat freezes, combine the remaining ingredients in a small saucepan. Place over medium heat and stir until the sugar dissolves. Let cool, then carefully pour over the strips in the bag. Squish everything around to coat, then seal the bag and refrigerate until the meat is no longer red, about 24 hours, turning and squishing the bag about halfway through to ensure even coverage with the marinade.
3. Drain off the marinade and place the strips in a single layer on dehydrator rack.
4. Push in the legs on the Crisper Tray, then place the tray in the bottom position in the pot. Put the rack with jerk on the tray.
5. Close the lid and flip the SmartSwitch to AIRFRY/STOVETOP. Select DEHYDRATE, set temperature to 150°F, and set time to 6 hours. Press START/STOP to begin cooking. When done, the jerky should bend but not snap, and show no signs of redness.
6. Remove the jerky from the cooker, arrange on baking sheets in a single layer, and place in a preheated 275°F oven for 15 minutes. Allow the jerky to cool completely before placing in an airtight container.

Kiwi Fruit

Prep Time: 20 minutes, Cook Time: 8 hours, Serves: 6

spray bottle of lemon juice
6 medium kiwi fruits, peeled and sliced as thinly as you can

1. Lightly spray the kiwi slices with lemon juice, spread on dehydrator rack.

2. Push in the legs on the Crisper Tray, then place the tray in the bottom position in the pot. Put the rack with kiwi slices on the tray.

3. Close the lid and flip the SmartSwitch to AIRFRY/STOVETOP. Select DEHYDRATE, set temperature to 135°F, and set time to 8 hours. Press START/STOP to begin cooking. When done, the kiwi should feel dry like paper, be flexible, and tear easily.

4. Remove the kiwi from the cooker, place in ziptop plastic freezer bags and seal, trying to remove as much air as possible. Double-bag inside a Mylar bag, or store inside a canning jar with a lid and oxygen pack.

Mango

Prep Time: 20 minutes, Cook Time: 8 hours, Serves: 4

spray bottle of lemon juice   4 large mangoes

1. Peel the mangoes; then, from top to bottom, cut the flesh off the large, flat seed on both sides. Cut the large pieces into wedges, or thinly slice if making mango chips, or chop. Lightly spray with lemon juice. Spread on dehydrator rack.

2. Push in the legs on the Crisper Tray, then place the tray in the bottom position in the pot. Put the rack with mango on the tray.

3. Close the lid and flip the SmartSwitch to AIRFRY/STOVETOP. Select DEHYDRATE, set temperature to 135°F, and set time to 8 hours. Press START/STOP to begin cooking. When done, the mango should feel dry like paper, be flexible, and tear easily.

4. Remove the mango from the cooker, serve immediately ou vacuum seal in vacuum bags with an oxygen pack, and then double-bagged in Mylar bag.

Dragon Fruit

Prep Time: 20 minutes, Cook Time: 6 hours, Serves: 6

3 large Dragon Fruits, washed thoroughly, cut into ¼-inch slices and left the skin on the fruit (can hold the slices together)

1. Spread the fruit slices on dehydrator rack.

2. Push in the legs on the Crisper Tray, then place the tray in the bottom position in the pot. Put the rack with fruit slices on the tray.

3. Close the lid and flip the SmartSwitch to AIRFRY/STOVETOP. Select DEHYDRATE, set temperature to 135°F, and set time to 6 hours. Press START/STOP to begin cooking. When done, the fruit slices should feel dry like paper, be flexible, and tear easily.

4. Remove the fruit slices from the cooker, serve immediately ou vacuum seal in vacuum bags with an oxygen pack, and then double-bagged in Mylar bag.

Olives

Prep Time: 10 minutes, Cook Time: 8 hours, Serves: 6

1 pounds green olives, drained and pitted

1. Spread the olives on dehydrator rack.
2. Push in the legs on the Crisper Tray, then place the tray in the bottom position in the pot. Put the rack with olives on the tray.
3. Close the lid and flip the SmartSwitch to AIRFRY/STOVETOP. Select DEHYDRATE, set temperature to 135°F, and set time to 8 hours. Press START/STOP to begin cooking. When done, the olives should feel dry like paper and be somewhat flexible but will snap if bent in half.
4. Remove the olives from the cooker, serve immediately ou vacuum seal in vacuum bags with an oxygen pack, and then double-bagged in Mylar bag.

Strawberries

Prep Time: 20 minutes, Cook Time: 7 hours, Serves: 6

spray bottle of lemon juice   1 pounds strawberries, washed and hulled, then thin sliced

1. Lightly spray the strawberries with lemon juice. Spread on dehydrator rack.
2. Push in the legs on the Crisper Tray, then place the tray in the bottom position in the pot. Put the rack with strawberries on the tray.
3. Close the lid and flip the SmartSwitch to AIRFRY/STOVETOP. Select DEHYDRATE, set temperature to 135°F, and set time to 7 hours. Press START/STOP to begin cooking. When done, the strawberries should feel dry like paper and be somewhat flexible.
4. Remove the strawberries from the cooker, serve immediately ou vacuum seal in vacuum bags with an oxygen pack, and then double-bagged in Mylar bag.

Asparagus

Prep Time: 20 minutes, Cook Time: 8 hours, Serves: 6

1 pounds asparagus, washed

1. Remove the tough end, then boil or steam asparagus just until you can pierce the thick end with a knife; don't let it get mushy. Drain, then plunge into a large bowl of ice water until cool. Cut thick stalks into 1- to 3-inch pieces; thin stalks can be left whole. Spread on dehydrator rack.
2. Push in the legs on the Crisper Tray, then place the tray in the bottom position in the pot. Put the rack with asparagus on the tray.
3. Close the lid and flip the SmartSwitch to AIRFRY/STOVETOP. Select DEHYDRATE, set temperature to 135°F, and set time to 8 hours. Press START/STOP to begin cooking. When done, the asparagus should feel dry like paper and be somewhat flexible.
4. Remove the asparagus from the cooker, serve immediately ou vacuum seal in vacuum bags with an oxygen pack, and then double-bagged in Mylar bag.

Carrots

Prep Time: 15 minutes, Cook Time: 8 hours, Serves: 6

spray bottle of lemon juice
1 pounds carrots, trimmed and peeled

1. Blanch carrots in a large pot of boiling water for 5 minutes, and no longer (they are ready when they turn bright orange). Drain and place in a large bowl of ice water to cool. Cut the carrots into ½-inch slices. Lightly spray with lemon juice, spread on dehydrator rack.
2. Push in the legs on the Crisper Tray, then place the tray in the bottom position in the pot. Put the rack with carrots on the tray.
3. Close the lid and flip the SmartSwitch to AIRFRY/STOVETOP. Select DEHYDRATE, set temperature to 135°F, and set time to 8 hours. Press START/STOP to begin cooking. When done, the carrots should feel hard and dry to the touch, but still be somewhat flexible.
4. Remove the carrots from the cooker, serve immediately ou vacuum seal in vacuum bags with an oxygen pack, and then double-bagged in Mylar bag.

Eggplant

Prep Time: 15 minutes, Cook Time: 6 hours, Serves: 6

1 pounds eggplants, washed and peeled

1. Blanch the entire eggplant in a large pot of boiling water for 15 seconds or less, then transfer it to a large bowl of ice water until cool. Cut the eggplant into ¼-inch slices, then spread on dehydrator rack.
2. Push in the legs on the Crisper Tray, then place the tray in the bottom position in the pot. Put the rack with eggplant on the tray.
3. Close the lid and flip the SmartSwitch to AIRFRY/STOVETOP. Select DEHYDRATE, set temperature to 135°F, and set time to 6 hours. Press START/STOP to begin cooking. When done, the eggplant should be brittle, feel dry to the touch, and snap in half.
4. Remove the eggplant from the cooker, serve immediately ou vacuum seal in vacuum bags with an oxygen pack, and then double-bagged in Mylar bag.

Tomatoes

Prep Time: 20 minutes, Cook Time: 6 hours, Serves: 6

1 pounds large tomatoes, washed and cut into ¼-inch slices

1. Spread the tomato slices on dehydrator rack.
2. Push in the legs on the Crisper Tray, then place the tray in the bottom position in the pot. Put the rack with tomatoes on the tray.
3. Close the lid and flip the SmartSwitch to AIRFRY/STOVETOP. Select DEHYDRATE, set temperature to 135°F, and set time to 6 hours. Press START/STOP to begin cooking. When done, the tomatoes should feel dry like paper, and be flexible but easily torn.
4. Remove the tomatoes from the cooker, serve immediately ou vacuum seal in vacuum bags with an oxygen pack, and then double-bagged in Mylar bag.

Brussels Sprouts

Prep Time: 20 minutes, Cook Time: 8 hours, Serves: 6

1 pounds Brussels sprouts, trimmed and removed any wilted leaves

1. Boil or steam whole Brussels sprouts until you can pierce them with a sharp knife or skewer. Drain and place the sprouts in a large bowl of ice water until cool. Cut each sprout vertically in half through the stem and spread on dehydrator rack, cut side up.

2. Push in the legs on the Crisper Tray, then place the tray in the bottom position in the pot. Put the rack with Brussels sprouts on the tray.

3. Close the lid and flip the SmartSwitch to AIRFRY/STOVETOP. Select DEHYDRATE, set temperature to 135°F, and set time to 8 hours. Press START/STOP to begin cooking. When done, the Brussels sprouts should feel dry to the touch and be crunchy.

4. Remove the Brussels sprouts from the cooker, serve immediately ou vacuum seal in vacuum bags with an oxygen pack, and then double-bagged in Mylar bag.

Spicy Sriracha Turkey Jerky

Prep Time: 15 minutes, Cook Time: 7 hours 15 minutes, Makes: ½ pound jerky

1½ pounds boneless, skinless turkey breast, trimmed of all visible fat

⅔ cup soy sauce   3 tbsps. honey

¼ cup sriracha 2 tsps. red pepper flakes

1. Partially freeze the turkey breast, then cut into ¼-inch-thick slices or strips using a very sharp knife or meat slicer. Try to cut it as uniformly as possible for even drying. Place the strips in a large ziptop plastic freezer bag.

2. Whisk the remaining ingredients together in a small bowl and carefully pour over the strips in the bag. Squish everything around to coat, then seal the bag and refrigerate for 12 hours, turning and squishing the bag about halfway through to ensure even coverage with the marinade.

3. Drain off the marinade and place the strips in a single layer on dehydrator rack. Push in the legs on the Crisper Tray, then place the tray in the bottom position in the pot. Put the rack with jerk on the tray.

4. Close the lid and flip the SmartSwitch to AIRFRY/STOVETOP. Select DEHYDRATE, set temperature to 150°F, and set time to 7 hours. Press START/STOP to begin cooking. When done, the jerky should bend but not snap.

5. Remove the jerky from the cooker, arrange on baking sheets in a single layer, and place in a preheated 275°F oven for 15 minutes. Allow the jerky to cool completely before placing in an airtight container.

Smoky Salmon Jerky

Prep Time: 30 minutes, Cook Time: 7 hours 15 minutes, Makes: ½ pound jerky

1½ pounds salmon fillets, skin and pin bones removed

½ cup soy sauce   1 tbsp. molasses

1 tbsp. lemon juice

1 tbsp. Worcestershire sauce

2 tsps. black pepper   1 tsp. liquid smoke

1. Partially freeze the fillets, then cut across into ¼- to ½-inch-thick slices or strips using a very sharp knife or meat slicer. Try to cut the salmon as uniformly as possible for even drying. Place the strips in a large ziptop plastic freezer bag.

2. Whisk the remaining ingredients together in a small bowl and carefully pour over the strips in the bag. Squish everything around to coat, then seal the bag and refrigerate for 3 to 6 hours (no longer, or you run the risk of the salmon becoming mushy), turning and squishing the bag about halfway through to ensure even coverage with the marinade.

3. Drain off the marinade and place the strips in a single layer on dehydrator rack.

4. Push in the legs on the Crisper Tray, then place the tray in the bottom position in the pot. Put the rack with jerk on the tray.

5. Close the lid and flip the SmartSwitch to AIRFRY/STOVETOP. Select DEHYDRATE, set temperature to 165°F, and set time to 7 hours. Press START/STOP to begin cooking. When done, the jerky should bend but not snap.

6. Remove the jerky from the cooker, arrange on baking sheets in a single layer, and place in a preheated 275°F oven for 15 minutes. Allow the jerky to cool completely before placing in an airtight container.

Sweet and Sour Chicken Jerky

Prep Time: 20 minutes, Cook Time: 6 hours 15 minutes, Makes: ½ pound jerky

1½ pounds boneless, skinless chicken breasts, trimmed of all visible fat

¼ cup firmly packed brown sugar

¼ cup distilled white vinegar

¼ cup pineapple juice

1 tbsp. powdered dehydrated onions

4 fresh garlic cloves, peeled and crushed

1 tbsp. soy sauce

1. Partially freeze the chicken breasts, then cut into ¼-inch-thick slices or strips using a very sharp knife or meat slicer. Try to cut them as uniformly as possible for even drying. Place the strips in a large ziptop plastic freezer bag.

2. Whisk the remaining ingredients together in a small bowl and carefully pour over the strips in the bag. Squish everything around to coat, then seal the bag and refrigerate for at least 12 hours, turning and squishing the bag about halfway through to ensure even coverage with the marinade.

3. Drain off the marinade and place the strips in a single layer on dehydrator rack.

4. Push in the legs on the Crisper Tray, then place the tray in the bottom position in the pot. Put the rack with jerk on the tray.

5. Close the lid and flip the SmartSwitch to AIRFRY/STOVETOP. Select DEHYDRATE, set temperature to 150°F, and set time to 6 hours. Press START/STOP to begin cooking. When done, the jerky should bend but not snap.

6. Remove the jerky from the cooker, arrange on baking sheets in a single layer, and place in a preheated 275°F oven for 15 minutes. Allow the jerky to cool completely before placing in an airtight container.

SLOW COOKER

Honey Beets and Onions

Prep Time: 14 minutes, Cook Time: 6 hours, Serves: 10

2 tbsps. melted coconut oil   ½ tsp. salt   ⅓ cup lemon juice   4 garlic cloves, minced
10 medium beets, peeled and sliced   1 cup water   3 tbsps. cornstarch
3 red onions, chopped   ⅓ cup honey

1. Before getting started, be sure to remove the crisper tray.
2. Add the beets, onions, and garlic to the bottom of the pot.
3. Mix the honey, lemon juice, water, coconut oil, cornstarch, and salt in a medium bowl, until well combined. Add this mixture over the beets.
4. Close the lid and flip the SmartSwitch to AIRFRY/STOVETOP. Select SLOW COOK, set temperature to "Lo", and set time to 6 hours. Press START/STOP to begin cooking, until the beets are soft and the sauce has thickened.
5. Serve warm.

Moroccan Beef Tagine

Prep Time: 15 minutes, Cook Time: 8 hours, Serves: 8 to 10

1 (3-pound / 1.4-kg) grass-fed beef sirloin roast, cut   2 jalapeño peppers, minced
into 2-inch pieces   2 onions, chopped   1 cup beef stock
3 carrots, cut into chunks   6 garlic cloves, minced   2 tbsps. honey
1 cup chopped dates   2 tsps. ground cumin   1 tsp. ground turmeric

1. Before getting started, be sure to remove the crisper tray.
2. Add the onions, garlic, jalapeño peppers, carrots, and dates to the bottom of the pot.
3. In a small bowl, mix the beef stock, honey, cumin, and turmeric until combined well. Pour the mixture into the pot.
4. Close the lid and flip the SmartSwitch to AIRFRY/STOVETOP. Select SLOW COOK, set temperature to "Lo", and set time to 8 hours. Press START/STOP to begin cooking, until the beef is soft.
5. Enjoy!

Pork Chops and Carrot

Prep Time: 20 minutes, Cook Time: 8 hours, Serves: 8

8 (5-ounce / 142-g) pork chops
4 large carrots, peeled and cut into chunks
½ cup chicken stock   2 onions, chopped
3 garlic cloves, minced

3 tbsps. grated fresh ginger root
3 tbsps. honey   ½ tsp. ground ginger
½ tsp. salt
⅛ tsp. freshly ground black pepper

1. Before getting started, be sure to remove the crisper tray.
2. Mix the onions, garlic, and carrots in the bottom of the pot. Place the pork chops on top.
3. Mix the ginger root, honey, stock, ginger, salt, and pepper in a small bowl. Pour into the pot.
4. Close the lid and flip the SmartSwitch to AIRFRY/STOVETOP. Select SLOW COOK, set temperature to "Lo", and set time to 8 hours. Press START/STOP to begin cooking, until the pork is very soft.
5. Serve warm.

Jerk Chicken Thigh

Prep Time: 13 minutes, Cook Time: 8 hours, Serves: 6

10 (4-ounce / 113-g) boneless, skinless chicken thighs
3 onions, chopped   6 garlic cloves, minced
½ cup freshly squeezed orange juice

3 tbsps. grated fresh ginger root
2 tbsps. honey   1 tbsp. chili powder
1 tsp. ground red chili   ½ tsp. ground cloves
¼ tsp. ground allspice

1. Cut slashes across the chicken thighs so the flavorings can permeate.
2. Mix the honey, ginger root, ground chili, chili powder, cloves, and allspice in a small bowl. Gently rub this mixture into the chicken. Allow the chicken to stand while you make the vegetables.
3. Before getting started, be sure to remove the crisper tray.
4. Place the onions and garlic to the bottom of the pot. Then top with the chicken. Add the orange juice over all.
5. Close the lid and flip the SmartSwitch to AIRFRY/STOVETOP. Select SLOW COOK, set temperature to "Lo", and set time to 8 hours. Press START/STOP to begin cooking, until a food thermometer registers 165ºF (74ºC). Serve warm.

Healthy Root Veggies

Prep Time: 21 minutes, Cook Time: 8 hours, Serves: 11

6 large carrots, cut into chunks
3 sweet potatoes, peeled and cut into chunks
2 medium rutabagas, peeled and cut into chunks

2 onions, chopped   3 tbsps. honey
½ tsp. salt   ⅛ tsp. freshly ground black pepper

1. Before getting started, be sure to remove the crisper tray.
2. Mix all the ingredients in the bottom of the pot and gently stir.
3. Close the lid and flip the SmartSwitch to AIRFRY/STOVETOP. Select SLOW COOK, set temperature to "Lo", and set time to 8 hours. Press START/STOP to begin cooking, until the vegetables are soft.
4. Enjoy!

Lemony Pork Chops

Prep Time: 18 minutes, Cook Time: 7 hours, Serves: 4

8 (5-ounce / 142-g) bone-in pork loin chops
2 leeks, chopped
2 red bell peppers, stemmed, seeded, and chopped

1 cup chicken stock   ⅓ cup lemon juice
8 garlic cloves, sliced   1 tsp. dried thyme leaves
½ tsp. salt

1. Before getting started, be sure to remove the crisper tray.
2. Add the leeks, garlic, and red bell peppers to the bottom of the pot. Top with the pork chops.
3. In a small bowl, mix the chicken stock, thyme, lemon juice, and salt. Pour the mixture over the pork.
4. Close the lid and flip the SmartSwitch to AIRFRY/STOVETOP. Select SLOW COOK, set temperature to "Lo", and set time to 7 hours. Press START/STOP to begin cooking, until the chops register at least 145ºF (63ºC) on a food thermometer.
5. Serve warm.

Barbecue Chicken

Prep Time: 6 minutes, Cook Time: 7 hours, Serves: 4

8 (6-ounce / 170-g) boneless, skinless chicken breasts
2 (8-ounce / 227-g) BPA-free cans no-salt-added tomato sauce

⅓ cup mustard   2 onions, minced
8 garlic cloves, minced   3 tbsps. molasses
2 tbsps. lemon juice   1 tbsp. chili powder
2 tsps. paprika   ¼ tsp. cayenne pepper

1. Before getting started, be sure to remove the crisper tray.
2. Mix the tomato sauce, onions, garlic, mustard, lemon juice, molasses, chili powder, paprika, and cayenne in the bottom of the pot.
3. Place the chicken and move the chicken around in the sauce with tongs to coat.
4. Close the lid and flip the SmartSwitch to AIRFRY/STOVETOP. Select SLOW COOK, set temperature to "Lo", and set time to 7 hours. Press START/STOP to begin cooking, until the chicken registers 165ºF (74ºC) on a food thermometer.
5. Serve warm.

Honey Roasted Carrots and Parsnips

Prep Time: 11 minutes, Cook Time: 6 hours, Serves: 10

2 tbsps. olive oil
6 large carrots, peeled and cut into 2-inch pieces
5 large parsnips, peeled and cut into 2-inch pieces

2 red onions, chopped   4 garlic cloves, minced
1 tbsp. honey   ½ tsp. salt

1. Before getting started, be sure to remove the crisper tray.
2. Add all the ingredients to the bottom of the pot and stir gently.
3. Close the lid and flip the SmartSwitch to AIRFRY/STOVETOP. Select SLOW COOK, set temperature to "Lo", and set time to 6 hours. Press START/STOP to begin cooking, until the vegetables are soft.
4. Enjoy!

Classic Jambalaya

Prep Time: 20 minutes, Cook Time: 9½ hours, Serves: 6 to 8

1½ pounds (680 g) raw shrimp, shelled and deveined

10 (4-ounce / 113-g) boneless, skinless chicken thighs, cut into 2-inch pieces

5 celery stalks, sliced

2 jalapeño peppers, minced

2 green bell peppers, stemmed, seeded, and chopped

2 cups chicken stock   2 onions, chopped

6 garlic cloves, minced   1 tbsp. Cajun seasoning

¼ tsp. cayenne pepper

Directions

1. Before getting started, be sure to remove the crisper tray.

2. Mix the chicken, onions, garlic, jalapeños, bell peppers, celery, chicken stock, Cajun seasoning, and cayenne in the bottom of the pot.

3. Close the lid and flip the SmartSwitch to AIRFRY/STOVETOP. Select SLOW COOK, set temperature to "Lo", and set time to 9 hours. Press START/STOP to begin cooking, until the chicken registers 165ºF (74ºC) on a food thermometer.

4. Stir in the shrimp. Close the lid and cook on low for an additional 30 to 40 minutes, or until the shrimp are curled and pink. Serve warm.

Curried Chicken

Prep Time: 8 minutes, Cook Time: 8½ hours, Serves: 5

10 (4-ounce / 113-g) boneless, skinless chicken thighs

4 large tomatoes, seeded and chopped

⅔ cup canned coconut milk

½ cup plain Greek yogurt

⅓ cup lemon juice   2 onions, chopped

8 garlic cloves, sliced   5 tsps. curry powder

3 tbsps. cornstarch

2 tbsps. grated fresh ginger root

1. Mix the yogurt, lemon juice, curry powder, and ginger root in a medium bowl. Place the chicken and stir to coat well. Let stand for about 15 minutes while you make the other ingredients.

2. Before getting started, be sure to remove the crisper tray.

3. Mix the tomatoes, onions, and garlic in the bottom of the pot.

4. Place the chicken-yogurt mixture to the pot.

5. Close the lid and flip the SmartSwitch to AIRFRY/STOVETOP. Select SLOW COOK, set temperature to "Lo", and set time to 8 hours. Press START/STOP to begin cooking, until the chicken registers 165ºF (74ºC) on a food thermometer.

6. Mix the coconut milk and cornstarch in a small bowl. Stir the mixture into the pot.

7. Close the lid and cook on low for an additional 15 to 20 minutes, or until the sauce has thickened. Serve warm.

Thai Beef Roast and Veggies

Prep Time: 14 minutes, Cook Time: 9 hours, Serves: 10

2½ pounds (1.1 kg) grass-fed beef sirloin roast, cut into 2-inch pieces
3 large tomatoes, seeded and chopped
3 large carrots, shredded
3 onions, chopped   1 cup canned coconut milk

¾ cup peanut butter   6 garlic cloves, minced
½ cup beef stock
1 small red chili pepper, minced
2 tbsps. grated fresh ginger root
3 tbsps. lime juice

1. Before getting started, be sure to remove the crisper tray.
2. Mix the onions, garlic, carrots, ginger root, and tomatoes in the bottom of the pot.
3. In a medium bowl, mix the coconut milk, peanut butter, chili pepper, lime juice, and beef stock until blended well.
4. Place the roast on top of the vegetables in the pot and pour the peanut sauce over all.
5. Close the lid and flip the SmartSwitch to AIRFRY/STOVETOP. Select SLOW COOK, set temperature to "Lo", and set time to 9 hours. Press START/STOP to begin cooking, until the beef is very soft.
6. Serve warm.

Barley Risotto with Mushroom

Prep Time: 12 minutes, Cook Time: 7 hours, Serves: 6 to 8

1 (8-ounce / 227-g) package button mushrooms, chopped
2¼ cups hulled barley, rinsed
6 cups low-sodium vegetable broth
⅔ cup grated Parmesan cheese

1 onion, finely chopped
4 garlic cloves, minced
½ tsp. dried marjoram leaves
⅛ tsp. freshly ground black pepper

1. Before getting started, be sure to remove the crisper tray.
2. Mix the barley, onion, garlic, mushrooms, broth, marjoram, and pepper in the bottom of the pot.
3. Close the lid and flip the SmartSwitch to AIRFRY/STOVETOP. Select SLOW COOK, set temperature to "Lo", and set time to 7 hours. Press START/STOP to begin cooking, until the barley has absorbed most of the liquid and is soft, and the vegetables are tender.
4. Toss in the Parmesan cheese and serve warm.

Beef Roast and Mushroom

Prep Time: 16 minutes, Cook Time: 10 hours, Serves: 8 to 10

2 tbsps. butter
1 (3-pound / 1.4-kg) grass-fed chuck shoulder roast or tri-tip roast, cut into 2-inch pieces
5 large carrots, sliced
2 cups sliced cremini mushrooms

1 cup low-sodium beef broth   2 onions, sliced
4 garlic cloves, sliced
2 shallots, peeled and sliced
2 tbsps. chopped fresh chives
1 tsp. dried marjoram leaves

1. Before getting started, be sure to remove the crisper tray.
2. Mix the onions, garlic, shallots, mushrooms, and carrots in the bottom of the pot.
3. Place the beef and stir slowly. Scatter the chives and marjoram over the beef, and add the beef broth over all.
4. Close the lid and flip the SmartSwitch to AIRFRY/STOVETOP. Select SLOW COOK, set temperature to "Lo", and set time to 10 hours. Press START/STOP to begin cooking, until the beef is very soft.
5. Stir in the butter and serve warm.

Mustard Beef Brisket

Prep Time: 15 minutes, Cook Time: 10 hours, Serves: 12

1 (3-pound / 1.4-kg) grass-fed beef brisket, trimmed

2 (8-ounce / 227-g) BPA-free cans no-salt-added tomato sauce

⅓ cup natural mustard

3 onions, chopped   8 garlic cloves, minced

3 tbsps. honey   2 tsps. paprika

1 tsp. dried marjoram leaves

1 tsp. dried oregano leaves

½ tsp. cayenne pepper

1. Before getting started, be sure to remove the crisper tray.
2. Add the onions and garlic to the bottom of the pot.
3. In a small bowl, mix the oregano, marjoram, paprika, and cayenne. Gently rub this mixture into the beef brisket.
4. Mix the tomato sauce, mustard, and honey until well combined in another small bowl.
5. Place the beef on the onions and garlic in the pot. Add the tomato mixture over all.
6. Close the lid and flip the SmartSwitch to AIRFRY/STOVETOP. Select SLOW COOK, set temperature to "Lo", and set time to 10 hours. Press START/STOP to begin cooking, until the beef is very soft.
7. Slice or shred the beef and serve it on buns.

Salmon Vegetables Chowder

Prep Time: 15 minutes, Cook Time: 7½ hours, Serves: 8 to 10

2 pounds (907 g) skinless salmon fillets

6 medium Yukon Gold potatoes, cut into 2-inch pieces

4 large carrots, sliced   1 cup whole milk

2 cups sliced cremini mushrooms

1½ cups shredded Swiss cheese

8 cups vegetable broth or fish stock

4 shallots, minced   3 garlic cloves, minced

2 tsps. dried dill weed

1. Before getting started, be sure to remove the crisper tray.
2. Mix the potatoes, carrots, mushrooms, shallots, garlic, vegetable broth, and dill weed in the bottom of the pot.
3. Close the lid and flip the SmartSwitch to AIRFRY/STOVETOP. Select SLOW COOK, set temperature to "Lo", and set time to 7 hours. Press START/STOP to begin cooking, until the vegetables are soft.
4. Place the salmon fillets to the pot. Close the lid and cook on low for an additional 20 to 30 minutes, or until the salmon flakes when tested with a fork.
5. Gently stir the chowder to break up the salmon.
6. Pour in the milk and Swiss cheese and cover. Let the chowder sit for 10 minutes to let the cheese melt. Stir in the chowder and serve warm.

SOUS VIDE

Chicken Wings

Prep Time: 20 minutes, Cook Time: 2 hours, Serves: 4

12 chicken wings	¼ cup vegetable oil	2 tsps. crushed red pepper flakes
4 sprigs thyme	Salt, to taste	

1. Before getting started, remove the crisper tray and add 12 cups of room-temperature water to the pot (reference the marking on the inside of the pot).
2. Close the lid and flip the SmartSwitch to AIRFRY/STOVETOP. Select SOUS VIDE, set temperature to 165°F, and set time to 2 hours.
3. Press START/STOP to begin preheating.(Time for preheating depends on the temperature of the water added.).
4. In a Sous Vide bag, combine the chicken wing with remaining ingredients. Shake gently to coat the chicken.
5. When preheating is complete and "ADD FOOD" will show on the display.
6. Open the lid. Place the bag in water and seal it using the water displacement method.
7. Close the lid.
8. When cooking is complete, remove the bag with chicken from cooker.
9. Heat some oil in a large skillet.
10. Place the wings into a skillet and cook until the skin is crispy.
11. Serve.

Rare Duck Breast

Prep Time: 10 minutes, Cook Time: 2 hours, Serves: 2

2 duck breasts	¼ cup olive oil	4 sprigs thyme	Salt and pepper

1. Before getting started, remove the crisper tray and add 12 cups of room-temperature water to the pot (reference the marking on the inside of the pot).
2. Close the lid and flip the SmartSwitch to AIRFRY/STOVETOP. Select SOUS VIDE, set temperature to 135°F, and set time to 2 hours.
3. Press START/STOP to begin preheating.(Time for preheating depends on the temperature of the water added.).
4. Transfer the duck breast to a hot pan and sear them for 1-2 minutes per side.
5. Place in a zip bag with the olive oil and thyme.
6. When preheating is complete and "ADD FOOD" will show on the display.
7. Open the lid. Place the bag in water and seal it using the water displacement method.
8. Close the lid.
9. When cooking is complete, remove the bag with duck from cooker.
10. Sear them again for 1-2 minutes in a hot pan.
11. Allow them to rest and slice.
12. Sprinkle with salt and pepper and serve.

Coconut Chicken

Prep Time: 10 minutes, Cook Time: 1 hour, Serves: 2

2 chicken breasts   4 tbsps. coconut milk   **FOR SAUCE:**

Salt and pepper as needed

4 tbsps. satay sauce   2 tbsps. coconut milk

Dash fish sauce

1. Before getting started, remove the crisper tray and add 12 cups of room-temperature water to the pot (reference the marking on the inside of the pot).

2. Close the lid and flip the SmartSwitch to AIRFRY/STOVETOP. Select SOUS VIDE, set temperature to 165°F, and set time to 1 hour.

3. Press START/STOP to begin preheating.(Time for preheating depends on the temperature of the water added.).

4. Add the chicken in a zip bag and add the salt, pepper and 4 tbsps. of milk.

5. When preheating is complete and "ADD FOOD" will show on the display.

6. Open the lid. Place the bag in water and seal it using the water displacement method.

7. Close the lid.

8. Once done, mix the sauce ingredients in a bowl and microwave for 30 seconds

9. Slice the chicken and arrange on serving platter

10. Pour the sauce on top. Serve at once.

Garlic Shrimps

Prep Time: 10 minutes, Cook Time: 30 minutes, Serves: 4

16 shrimps, peeled and deveined   2 garlic cloves, minced

1 shallot, minced   **FOR SERVING:**

1 tbsp. unsalted butter, melted   penne pasta (optional)

1. Before getting started, remove the crisper tray and add 12 cups of room-temperature water to the pot (reference the marking on the inside of the pot).

2. Close the lid and flip the SmartSwitch to AIRFRY/STOVETOP. Select SOUS VIDE, set temperature to 130°F, and set time to 30 minutes.

3. Press START/STOP to begin preheating.(Time for preheating depends on the temperature of the water added.).

4. Put all the ingredients in a resealable bag.

5. When preheating is complete and "ADD FOOD" will show on the display.

6. Open the lid. Place the bag in water and seal it using the water displacement method.

7. Close the lid.

8. When the time is up, remove the bag with shrimp from cooker.

9. Serve immediately as an appetizer or tossed with penne pasta.

Panko Crusted Chicken

Prep Time: 30 minutes, Cook Time: 1 hour 30 minutes, Serves: 4

4 boneless chicken breasts   Canola oil   2 eggs   Salt and pepper
1 lb. sliced mushrooms Small bunch of thyme   1 cup panko bread crumbs

1. Before getting started, remove the crisper tray and add 12 cups of room-temperature water to the pot (reference the marking on the inside of the pot).
2. Close the lid and flip the SmartSwitch to AIRFRY/STOVETOP. Select SOUS VIDE, set temperature to 165°F, and set time to 1 hour 30 minutes.
3. Press START/STOP to begin preheating.(Time for preheating depends on the temperature of the water added.).
4. Season the chicken with salt, and thyme. Put the breast in a resealable bag.
5. When preheating is complete and "ADD FOOD" will show on the display.
6. Open the lid. Place the bag in water and seal it using the water displacement method.
7. Close the lid.
8. Then, place a pan over medium heat, add the mushrooms and cook them until the water has evaporated.
9. Add 3-4 sprigs of thyme and stir.
10. Once cooked, remove the chicken from the bag and pat dry.
11. Add the oil and heat it up over medium-high heat. Add the eggs into a container and dip the chicken in egg wash until well coated.
12. Add the panko bread crumbs in a shallow container and add some salt and pepper. Put the chicken to bread crumbs and coat until well covered.
13. Fry the chicken for 1-2 minutes per side and serve with the mushrooms.

New York Strip Steak

Prep Time: 5 minutes, Cook Time: 1 hour, Serves: 1

1 New York Strip Steak   Steak seasoning as you prefer
Salt and pepper as needed   Rosemary and thyme
Olive oil

1. Before getting started, remove the crisper tray and add 12 cups of room-temperature water to the pot (reference the marking on the inside of the pot).
2. Close the lid and flip the SmartSwitch to AIRFRY/STOVETOP. Select SOUS VIDE, set temperature to 145°F, and set time to 1 hour.
3. Press START/STOP to begin preheating.(Time for preheating depends on the temperature of the water added.).
4. Season the steak with pepper and salt and place the herbs on top. Add it in a zip bag.
5. When preheating is complete and "ADD FOOD" will show on the display.
6. Open the lid. Place the bag in water and seal it using the water displacement method.
7. Close the lid.
8. Once done, remove from the bag and pat dry the steak.
9. Drizzle olive oil over and season.
10. Grill for 1 minute (each side) at 400ºF.
11. Slice and serve!

Pulled Pork

Prep Time: 10 minutes, Cook Time: 24 hours, Serves: 6

2 lbs. pork shoulder, trimmed   1 tbsp. ketchup   syrup
4 tbsps. Dijon mustard   2   tbsps.   maple   2 tbsps. soy sauce

1. Before getting started, remove the crisper tray and add 12 cups of room-temperature water to the pot (reference the marking on the inside of the pot).

2. Close the lid and flip the SmartSwitch to AIRFRY/STOVETOP. Select SOUS VIDE, set temperature to 165°F, and set time to 24 hours.

3. Press START/STOP to begin preheating.(Time for preheating depends on the temperature of the water added.).

4. In a bowl, combine ketchup, mustard, maple syrup, and soy sauce.

5. Wrap the pork with prepared sauce in plastic wrap, then put into Sous Vide bag.

6. When preheating is complete and "ADD FOOD" will show on the display.

7. Open the lid. Place the bag in water and seal it using the water displacement method.

8. Close the lid.

9. When cooking is complete, open the bag and remove pork.

10. Strain cooking juices into a saucepan. Torch the pork to create a crust.

11. Simmer the cooking juices in a saucepan until thickened.

12. Pull pork before serving.

13. Serve with thickened sauce.

BBQ Pork

Prep Time: 5 minutes, Cook Time: 3 hours, Serves: 4

1 pound pork tenderloin   Salt and pepper to taste ¼ cup BBQ sauce
2 garlic cloves, coarsely chopped   1 tbsp dried oregano   ½ tsp liquid smoke
2 tbsp garlic powder   2 tbsp ground paprika

1. Before getting started, remove the crisper tray and add 12 cups of room-temperature water to the pot (reference the marking on the inside of the pot).

2. Close the lid and flip the SmartSwitch to AIRFRY/STOVETOP. Select SOUS VIDE, set temperature to 145°F, and set time to 3 hours.

3. Press START/STOP to begin preheating.(Time for preheating depends on the temperature of the water added.).

4. Mix salt, pepper, garlic powder, paprika and oregano in a bowl.

5. Rub the pork with the spice mixture and put it into Sous Vide bag.

6. Add 1 garlic clove to the bag.

7. When preheating is complete and "ADD FOOD" will show on the display.

8. Open the lid. Place the bag in water and seal it using the water displacement method.

9. Close the lid.

10. When the time is up, carefully removing the pork from the bag. In a saucepan, sear it on both sides over the high heat with 1 tbsp olive oil until light brown.

11. Slice the pork and serve with the BBQ sauce.

Hoisin Glazed Pork Tenderloin

Prep Time: 20 minutes, Cook Time: 3 hours, Serves: 3

1-piece pork tenderloin, trimmed

1 tsp. kosher salt

½ tsp. freshly ground black pepper

3 tbsps. hoisin sauce

1. Before getting started, remove the crisper tray and add 12 cups of room-temperature water to the pot (reference the marking on the inside of the pot).
2. Close the lid and flip the SmartSwitch to AIRFRY/STOVETOP. Select SOUS VIDE, set temperature to 145°F, and set time to 3 hours.
3. Press START/STOP to begin preheating.(Time for preheating depends on the temperature of the water added.).
4. Take the tenderloins and season it with pepper and salt and transfer to a resealable zip bag.
5. When preheating is complete and "ADD FOOD" will show on the display.
6. Open the lid. Place the bag in water and seal it using the water displacement method.
7. Close the lid.
8. When the time is up, remove the bag and then the pork, brush with hoisin sauce.
9. Heat up your grill to high grill and add the tenderloin, sear for 5 minutes until all sides are caramelized.
10. Allow it to rest and slice the tenderloin into medallions, serve!

Beer Braised Pork Ribs

Prep Time: 10 minutes, Cook Time: 18 hours, Serves: 4

2 pounds pork ribs, chopped into bone sections

1 big onion, finely chopped

12 ounce can light beer

Salt and pepper to taste   1 tbsp. butter

FOR SERVING:

mashed potatoes, coleslaw or white rice

1. Before getting started, remove the crisper tray and add 12 cups of room-temperature water to the pot (reference the marking on the inside of the pot).
2. Close the lid and flip the SmartSwitch to AIRFRY/STOVETOP. Select SOUS VIDE, set temperature to 165°F, and set time to 18 hours.
3. Press START/STOP to begin preheating.(Time for preheating depends on the temperature of the water added.).
4. Rub the pork ribs with salt and pepper.
5. Double-bag the ribs with chopped onion and beer, then put into Sous Vide bag.
6. When preheating is complete and "ADD FOOD" will show on the display.
7. Open the lid. Place the bag in water and seal it using the water displacement method.
8. Close the lid.
9. When the time is up, carefully dry the ribs with the paper towels.
10. In a saucepan, sear the ribs in 1 tbsp. butter on both sides for about 40 seconds until crusty.
11. Serve with mashed potatoes, coleslaw or white rice.

Miso Butter Cod

Prep Time: 15 minutes, Cook Time: 30 minutes, Serves: 2

1 large Atlantic Cod fillet

2 tbsps. miso paste

1½ tbsps. brown sugar

2 tbsps. soy sauce

2 tbsps. mirin

Sesame seeds for garnishing

steamed rice for serving

2 tbsps. butter

1. Before getting started, remove the crisper tray and add 12 cups of room-temperature water to the pot (reference the marking on the inside of the pot).
2. Close the lid and flip the SmartSwitch to AIRFRY/STOVETOP. Select SOUS VIDE, set temperature to 130°F, and set time to 30 minutes.
3. Press START/STOP to begin preheating.(Time for preheating depends on the temperature of the water added.).
4. Marinate the cod with the brown sugar, miso paste, mirin and soy sauce mixture.
5. Transfer the fish to a heavy-duty sous vide zip bag.
6. When preheating is complete and "ADD FOOD" will show on the display.
7. Open the lid. Place the bag in water and seal it using the water displacement method.
8. Close the lid.
9. When the time is up, remove the bag with cod from cooker.
10. Place a pan over the medium heat. Add in 1 tbsp. of butter.
11. Sear the cod for 1 minute and pour the juices from the bag into the pan.
12. Reduce until it thickened and add 1 tbsp. of butter on top and stir.
13. Drizzle the sauce onto the cod and garnish with some sesame seeds.
14. Serve over steamed rice!

Fingerling Cooked Potatoes

Prep Time: 10 minutes, Cook Time: 45 minutes, Serves: 3

8 ounces fingerling potatoes

Salt, and pepper to taste

1 tbsp. unsalted vegan butter

1 sprig rosemary

1. Before getting started, remove the crisper tray and add 12 cups of room-temperature water to the pot (reference the marking on the inside of the pot).
2. Close the lid and flip the SmartSwitch to AIRFRY/STOVETOP. Select SOUS VIDE, set temperature to 190°F, and set time to 45 minutes.
3. Press START/STOP to begin preheating.(Time for preheating depends on the temperature of the water added.).
4. Take the potatoes and season it with salt and pepper and transfer them to a resealable zip bag.
5. When preheating is complete and "ADD FOOD" will show on the display.
6. Open the lid. Place the bag in water and seal it using the water displacement method.
7. Close the lid.
8. Once cooked, remove the bag with potatoes.
9. Cut the potatoes in half (lengthwise).
10. Take a large skillet and put it over medium-high heat.
11. Add the butter and allow it to melt, add the rosemary and potatoes.
12. Cook for 3 minutes and transfer to a plate.
13. Serve by seasoning it with a bit of salt if needed.

Daikon Radishes

Prep Time: 10 minutes, Cook Time: 30 minutes, Serves: 4

½ cup white winger vinegar
3 tbsps. beet sugar   2 tsps. kosher salt

1 large size Daikon radish, trimmed and sliced up

1. Before getting started, remove the crisper tray and add 12 cups of room-temperature water to the pot (reference the marking on the inside of the pot).
2. Close the lid and flip the SmartSwitch to AIRFRY/STOVETOP. Select SOUS VIDE, set temperature to 180°F, and set time to 30 minutes.
3. Press START/STOP to begin preheating.(Time for preheating depends on the temperature of the water added.).
4. Mix vinegar, salt, and beet sugar in a large bowl. Transfer to a Sous-vide zip bag.
5. When preheating is complete and "ADD FOOD" will show on the display.
6. Open the lid. Place the bag in water and seal it using the water displacement method.
7. Close the lid.
8. Once cooked, remove the bag and transfer to an ice bath.
9. Serve!

Honey Drizzled Carrots

Prep Time: 5 minutes, Cook Time: 45 minutes, Serves: 4

1 pound baby carrots   4 tbsps. vegan butter   ¼ tsp. kosher salt   ¼ tsp. ground cardamom
1 tbsp. agave nectar   3 tbsps. honey

1. Before getting started, remove the crisper tray and add 12 cups of room-temperature water to the pot (reference the marking on the inside of the pot).
2. Close the lid and flip the SmartSwitch to AIRFRY/STOVETOP. Select SOUS VIDE, set temperature to 180°F, and set time to 45 minutes.
3. Press START/STOP to begin preheating.(Time for preheating depends on the temperature of the water added.).
4. Add the carrots, honey, whole butter, kosher salt, and cardamom to a resealable bag.
5. When preheating is complete and "ADD FOOD" will show on the display.
6. Open the lid. Place the bag in water and seal it using the water displacement method.
7. Close the lid.
8. Once done, remove the bag with carrots from cooker.
9. Strain the glaze by passing through a fine mesh.
10. Set it aside.
11. Take the carrots out from the bag and pour any excess glaze over them. Serve with a little bit of seasonings.

Thai Tom Yum Fish

Prep Time: 10 minutes, Cook Time: 1 hour, Serves: 2

2 medium fish fillets
2 tbsps. Tom Yum paste

FOR SERVING:
white rice   Fresh cilantro
1 tbsp. lime juice

1. Before getting started, remove the crisper tray and add 12 cups of room-temperature water to the pot (reference the marking on the inside of the pot).
2. Close the lid and flip the SmartSwitch to AIRFRY/STOVETOP. Select SOUS VIDE, set temperature to 130°F, and set time to 1 hour.
3. Press START/STOP to begin preheating.(Time for preheating depends on the temperature of the water added.).
4. Rub the fillets with the Tom Yum paste, and put them into a resealable bag.
5. When preheating is complete and "ADD FOOD" will show on the display.
6. Open the lid. Place the bag in water and seal it using the water displacement method.
7. Close the lid.
8. When cooking is complete, remove the bag with fish from cooker.
9. Serve over white rice sprinkled with lime juice and topped with freshly chopped cilantro.

Steam & Crisp Chart

INGREDIENT	AMOUNT	PREPARATION	WATER	ORIENTATION	TEMP	COOK TIME
VEGETABLES						
Acorn squash	1	Cut in half, placed face down	½ cup	Bottom	390°F	15 mins
Beets	2½ lbs	Cut in 1-in pieces	½ cup	Bottom	400°F	30–35 mins
Broccoli	1 head	Whole, stem removed	½ cup	Bottom	400°F	10-15 mins
Brussels sprouts	2 lbs	Cut in half, ends trimmed	½ cup	Bottom	450°F	15–20 mins
Carrots	1 lb	Cut in 1-in pieces	½ cup	Bottom	400°F	20–25 mins
Cauliflower	1 head	Whole, stems removed	½ cup	Bottom	425°F	20–25 mins
Parsnip	2½ lbs	Cut in 1-in pieces	½ cup	Bottom	400°F	30–35 mins
Potatoes, russet	2 lbs	Cut in 1-in wedges	½ cup	Bottom	450°F	25–30 mins
	2 lbs	Hand-cut fries, soaked 30 mins in cold water then patted dry	½ cup	Bottom	450°F	30–35 mins
	4	Whole (medium), poked several times with a fork	1 cup	Bottom	400°F	30–35 mins
		Whole (large), poked several times with a fork	1 cup	Bottom	400°F	40–48 mins
	2½ lbs	Cut in 1-in pieces	½ cup	Bottom	450°F	30–35 mins
Spaghetti squash	1 small squash	Cut in half, deseeded, punctured with fork about 10 times	2 cups	Bottom	375°F	25–30 mins
Sweet potatoes	2½ lbs	Cut in 1-in pieces	½ cup	Bottom	450°F	20–25 mins
POULTRY						
Whole chicken	4½–5 lbs	Trussed	1 cup	Bottom	400°F	40–50 mins
Turkey drumstricks	2 lbs	None	1 cup	Bottom	400°F	32–38 mins
Turkey breast	1 (3–5 lbs)	None	1 cup	Bottom	365°F	45–55 mins
Chicken breasts (boneless)	4 breasts, 6–8 oz each	Brush with oil	½ cup	Elevated	390°F	15–20 mins
Chicken breasts (bone in, skin on)	4 breasts, ¾–1½ lbs	Brush with oil	½ cup	Elevated	375°F	20–25 mins
Chicken thighs (bone in)	4 thighs, 6–10 oz each	Brush with oil	½ cup	Elevated	400°F	20–25 mins
Chicken thighs (boneless)	6 thighs, 4–8 oz each	Brush with oil	½ cup	Elevated	375°F	15–18 mins
Chicken drumsticks	2 lbs	Brush with oil	½ cup	Elevated	425°F	20–25 mins
Hand-breaded chicken breasts	4 breasts, 6 oz each		½ cup	Elevated	385°F	18–20 mins
Chicken wings	2 lbs		½ cup	Bottom	450°F	20–25 mins
PORK						
Pork tenderloins	2 (1 lb each)	None	1 cup	Elevated	375°F	25–30 mins
Pork loin	1 (2 lbs)	None	1 cup	Elevated	365°F	35–40 mins
Spiral ham, bone in	1 (3 lbs)	None	1 cup	Elevated	325°F	45–50 mins
Pork chops, boneless	4 chops, 6–8 oz each	None	½ cup	Bottom	375°F	15-20 mins
Pork chops (bone in, thick cut)	2 chops, 10–12 oz each		½ cup	Bottom	375°F	25–30 mins

*NOTE: Crisper tray position varies, as specified in chart. Steam will take approximately 4–8 minutes to build.

Steam & Crisp Chart

INGREDIENT	AMOUNT	PREPARATION	WATER	ORIENTATION	TEMP	COOK TIME
FISH						
Cod	4 fillets, 6 oz each		½ cup	Elevated	450°F	9–12 mins
Salmon	4 fillets, 6 oz each		¼ cup	Elevated	450°F	7–10 mins
Scallops	1 lb (approx. 21 pieces)		¼ cup	Elevated	400°F	4–6 mins
BEEF						
Roast beef	2–3 lbs	None	1 cup	Bottom	360°F	45 mins for medium rare
Tenderloin	2–3 lbs	None	1 cup	Bottom	365°F	25–30 mins for medium rare
FROZEN CHICKEN						
Chicken Breasts, Boneless, Skinless	4 breasts, 4–6 oz each	As desired	½ cup	Elevated	390°F	20–25 mins
Chicken Thighs, Boneless, Skinless	6 thighs, 4–8 oz each	As desired	½ cup	Elevated	375°F	15–20 mins
Chicken Thighs, Bone-in Skin on	4 thighs, 8–10 oz each	As desired	½ cup	Elevated	400°F	20–25 mins
Pre-Breaded Chicken Breasts	3–4 breasts, 10–16 oz each	As desired	½ cup	Elevated	375°F	10–15 mins
Chicken Wings	2 lbs	As desired	½ cup	Bottom	450°F	25–30 mins
FROZEN BEEF						
NY Strip Steak	2 steaks, 10–14 oz each	2 tbsp canola oil, salt, pepper	¾ cup	Bottom	400°F	22–28 mins
FROZEN FISH						
Salmon	4 fillets, 6 oz each		½ cup	Elevated	450°F	11–15 mins
Shrimp	18 shrimp, 1 lb		½ cup	Bottom	450°F	2–5 mins
Cod	4 fillets, 6 oz each		½ cup	Elevated	450°F	10–15 mins
Lobster tails	4		½ cup	Elevated	450°F	5–7 mins
FROZEN PORK						
Pork tenderloins	2 (1 lb each)	None	1½ cups	Bottom	365°F	30–35 mins
Pork loin	1 (2 lbs)	None	None	Bottom	360°F	37–40 mins
Pork chops, boneless	4, 6–8 oz each		½ cup	Elevated	375°F	15–20 mins
Pork Chops, bone-in, thick cut	2, 10–12 oz each		¾ cup	Elevated	365°F	23–28 mins
Italian sausages	6 uncooked		½ cup	Elevated	375°F	10–12 mins
FROZEN PREPARED FOODS						
Dumplings/Pot stickers	16 oz bag		½ cup	Bottom	400°F	12–16 mins
Ravioli	25 oz bag		½ cup	Bottom	385°F	12–16 mins
Eggrolls	10 oz pkg		½ cup	Bottom	375°F	15–20 mins

*NOTE: Crisper tray position varies, as specified in chart. Steam will take approximately 4–8 minutes to build.

Air Fry Chart for the Crisper Tray, bottom position

INGREDIENT	AMOUNT	PREPARATION	OIL	TEMP	COOK TIME
VEGETABLES					
Asparagus	1 bunch	Cut in half, trim stems	2 tsp	390°F	8–10 mins
Beets	6 small or 4 large (about 2 lbs)	Whole	None	390°F	45–60 mins
Bell peppers	4 peppers	Whole	None	400°F	25–30 mins
Broccoli	1 head	Cut in 1–2-inch florets	1 Tbsp	390°F	10–13 mins
Brussels sprouts	1 lb	Cut in half, remove stems	1 Tbsp	390°F	15–18 mins
Butternut squash	1–1½ lbs	Cut in 1–2-inch pieces	1 Tbsp	390°F	20–25 mins
Carrots	1 lb	Peeled, cut in ½-inch pieces	1 Tbsp	390°F	14–16 mins
Cauliflower	1 head	Cut in 1–2-inch florets	2 Tbsp	390°F	15–20 mins
Corn on the cob	4 ears, cut in half	Whole, remove husks	1 Tbsp	390°F	12–15 mins
Green beans	1 bag (12 oz)	Trimmed	1 Tbsp	390°F	7–10 mins
Kale (for chips)	6 cups, packed	Tear in pieces, remove stems	None	300°F	8–11 mins
Mushrooms	8 oz	Rinse, cut in quarters	1 Tbsp	390°F	7–8 mins
Potatoes, russet	1½ lbs	Cut in 1-inch wedges	1 Tbsp	390°F	20–25 mins
	1 lb	Hand-cut fries, thin	½–3 Tbsp	390°F	20–25 mins
	1 lb	Hand-cut fries, soak 30 mins in cold water then pat dry	½–3 Tbsp	390°F	24–27 mins
	4 whole (6–8 oz)	Pierce with fork 3 times	None	390°F	35–40 mins
Potatoes, sweet	2 lbs	Cut in 1-inch chunks	1 Tbsp	390°F	15–20 mins
	4 whole (6–8 oz)	Pierce with fork 3 times	None	390°F	35–40 mins
Zucchini	1 lb	Cut in quarters lengthwise, then cut in 1-inch pieces	1 Tbsp	390°F	15–20 mins
POULTRY					
Chicken breasts	2 breasts (¾–1½ lbs each)	Bone in	Brushed with oil	375°F	25–35 mins
	2 breasts (½–¾ lb each)	Boneless	Brushed with oil	375°F	22–25 mins
Chicken thighs	4 thighs (6–10 oz each)	Bone in	Brushed with oil	390°F	22–28 mins
	4 thighs (4–8 oz each)	Boneless	Brushed with oil	390°F	18–22 mins
Chicken wings	2 lbs	Drumettes & flats	1 Tbsp	390°F	24–28 mins
Chicken, whole	1 chicken (4–6 lbs)	Trussed	Brushed with oil	375°F	55–75 mins
Chicken drumsticks	2 lbs	None	1 Tbsp	390°F	20–22 mins

*TIP When using Air Fry, add 5 minutes to the suggested cook time for the unit to preheat before you add ingredients.

Air Fry Chart for the Crisper Tray, bottom position

INGREDIENT	AMOUNT	PREPARATION	OIL	TEMP	COOK TIME
BEEF					
Burgers	4 quarter-pound patties, 80% lean	1-inch thick	None	375°F	10–12 mins
Steaks	2 steaks (8 oz each)	Whole	None	390°F	10–20 mins
PORK & LAMB					
Bacon	1 strip to 1 (16 oz) package	Lay strips evenly over the plate	None	330°F	13–16 mins (no preheat)
Pork chops	2 thick-cut, bone-in chops (10–12 oz each)	Bone in	Brushed with oil	375°F	15–17 mins
	4 boneless chops (6–8 oz each)	Boneless	Brushed with oil	375°F	15–18 mins
Pork tenderloins	2 tenderloins (1–1½ lbs each)	Whole	Brushed with oil	375°F	25–35 mins
Sausages	4 sausages	Whole	None	390°F	8–10 mins
FISH & SEAFOOD					
Crab cakes	2 cakes (6–8 oz each)	None	Brushed with oil	350°F	10–13 mins
Lobster tails	4 tails (3–4 oz each)	Whole	None	375°F	7–10 mins
Salmon fillets	2 fillets (4 oz each)	None	Brushed with oil	390°F	10–13 mins
Shrimp	16 jumbo	Raw, whole, peel, keep tails on	1 Tbsp	390°F	7–10 mins
FROZEN FOODS					
Chicken nuggets	1 box (12 oz)	None	None	390°F	11–13 mins
Fish fillets	1 box (6 fillets)	None	None	390°F	13–15 mins
Fish sticks	1 box (14.8 oz)	None	None	390°F	9–11 mins
French fries	1 lb	None	None	360°F	18–22 mins
	2 lbs	None	None	360°F	28–32 mins
Mozzarella sticks	1 box (11 oz)	None	None	375°F	6–9 mins
Pot stickers	1 bag (10 count)	None	Toss with 1 tsp oil	390°F	11–14 mins
Pizza Rolls	1 bag (20 oz, 40 count)	None	None	390°F	12–15 mins
Popcorn shrimp	1 box (16 oz)	None	None	390°F	8–10 mins
Tater Tots	1 lb	None	None	360°F	19–22 mins

*TIP When using Air Fry, add 5 minutes to the suggested cook time for the unit to preheat before you add ingredients.

Dehydrate Chart   for the Crisper Tray, bottom position

INGREDIENT	PREPARATION	TEMP	DEHYDRATE TIME
FRUITS & VEGETABLES			
Apple chips	Cut in ⅛-inch slices (remove core), rinse in lemon water, pat dry	135°F	7–8 hrs
Asparagus	Cut in 1-inch pieces, blanch	135°F	6–8 hrs
Bananas	Peel, cut in 3/8-inch slices	135°F	8–10 hrs
Beet chips	Peel, cut in ⅛-inch slices	135°F	7–8 hrs
Eggplant	Peel, cut in ¼-inch slices, blanch	135°F	6–8 hrs
Fresh herbs	Rinse, pat dry, remove stems	135°F	4–6 hrs
Ginger root	Cut in 3/8-inch slices	135°F	6 hrs
Mangoes	Peel, cut in 3/8-inch slices, remove pits	135°F	6–8 hrs
Mushrooms	Clean with soft brush (do not wash)	135°F	6–8 hrs
Pineapple	Peel, cut in 3/8–½-inch slices, core removed	135°F	6–8 hrs
Strawberries	Cut in half or in ½-inch slices	135°F	6–8 hrs
Tomatoes	Cut in 3/8-inch slices or grate; steam if planning to rehydrate	135°F	6–8 hrs
JERKY – MEAT, POULTRY, FISH			
Beef jerky	Cut in ¼-inch slices, marinate overnight	150°F	5–7 hrs
Chicken jerky	Cut in ¼-inch slices, marinate overnight	150°F	5–7 hrs
Turkey jerky	Cut in ¼-inch slices, marinate overnight	150°F	5–7 hrs
Salmon jerky	Cut in ¼-inch slices, marinate overnight	165°F	5–8 hrs

*TIP Most fruits and vegetables take between 6 and 8 hours (at 135°F) to dehydrate; meats take between 5 and 7 hours (at 150°F). The longer you dehydrate your ingredients, the crispier they will be.

Sous Vide Chart   Crisper Tray not used

INGREDIENT	AMOUNT	TEMP	COOK TIME
BEEF			
Boneless ribeye	2 steaks, 14 oz each, 1–2 inches thick	125°F Rare	1–5 hrs
Boneless ribeye	3 steaks, 14 oz each, 1–2 inches thick	130°F Medium Rare	1–5 hrs
		135°F Medium	1–5 hrs
Porterhouse	2 steaks, 14 oz each, 1–2 inches thick	145°F Medium Well	1–5 hrs
Filet mignon	4 steaks, 8 oz each, 1–2 inches thick	155°F Well Done	1–5 hrs
Flank	3 steaks, 12 oz each, 1–2 inches thick	125°F Rare	2–5 hrs
		130°F Medium Rare	2–5 hrs
		135°F Medium	2–5 hrs
Flat iron	2 steaks, 10 oz each, 1–2 inches thick	145°F Medium Well	2–5 hrs
		155°F Well Done	2–5 hrs
Beef brisket	3 lbs, 3–4 inches thick	145°F	24–48 hrs
PORK			
Boneless pork chops	5 chops, 6–8 oz each, 2½ inches thick	145°F	1–4 hrs
Bone-In pork chops	2 chops, 10–12 oz each, 2½ inches thick	145°F	1–4 hrs
Tenderloin	1 tenderloin, 1–1½ lbs, 2½ inches thick	145°F	1–4 hrs
Sausages	6 sausages, 2–3 oz each	165°F	2–5 hrs
Boneless pork shoulder	3 lbs, 3–4 inches thick	165°F	12–24 hrs
CHICKEN			
Chicken Breast	6 breasts, 6–8 oz each, 1–2 inches thick	165°F	1–3 hrs
Boneless Chicken Thighs	6 thighs, 4–6 oz each, 1–2 inches thick	165°F	1–3 hrs
Bone-In Chicken Thighs	4 thighs, 4–6 oz each, 1–2 inches thick	165°F	1½–4 hrs
Chicken Leg Quarters	2 quarters, 12–14 oz each, 1–2 inches thick	165°F	1½–4 hrs
Chicken Wings & Drummettes	2 lbs	165°F	1–3 hrs
Half Chicken	2½–3 lbs	165°F	2–3 hrs
SEAFOOD			
Whitefish (Cod, Haddock, Pollock)	2 portions, 6–10 oz each, 1–2 inches thick	130°F	1 hr–1½ hrs
Salmon	4 portions, 6–10 oz each, 1–2 inches thick	130°F	1 hr–1½ hrs
Shrimp	2 lbs	130°F	30 mins–2 hrs
VEGETABLES			
Asparagus	1–2 lbs	180°F	30 mins
Broccoli	1–1½ lbs	180°F	30 mins
Brussels Sprouts	1–2 lbs	180°F	45 mins
Carrots	1–1½ lbs	180°F	45 mins
Cauliflower	1–1½ lbs	180°F	30 mins
Green Beans	1–1½ lbs	180°F	30 mins
Squash	1–1½ lbs	185°F	1 hr
Sweet Potatoes	1–1½ lbs	185°F	1 hr
Potatoes	1–2 lbs	190°F	1 hr

*TIP Cook time is dependent on the weight as well as the thickness of food, so thicker cuts of meat will require longer cook times. If your ingredients are thicker than 2½ inches, add more time.

APPENDIX 2: RECIPES INDEX

Printed in Great Britain
by Amazon

22987339R00044